The Color Scanner Book

Stephen Beale and James Cavuoto

The Color Scanner Book
Stephen Beale and James Cavuoto

Published by:
Micro Publishing Press
21150 Hawthorne Blvd., Suite 104
Torrance, CA 90503
(310) 371-5787

First Printing, May, 1995

Printed in the United States of America

ISBN 0-941845-11-7

CONTENTS

Introduction 1

Chapter 1: An Introduction to Digital Imaging 7
Bits and Bytes 8
Color Perception 11
Color Models and Spaces 12
Continuous Tones Versus Halftones 17
Electronic Publishing Systems 19

Chapter 2: How Scanners Work 23
The Scanner's "Eyes" 24
Color Scanners 28
Scanning Mechanisms 30
Alternatives to Scanners 38

Chapter 3: Scanning Workstations 41
Host Computer 41
Hardware Interfaces 47
Memory Requirements 50
Graphics Displays 51
Mass Storage 53

Chapter 4: Capturing the Image 59
Types of Images 60
Scanner Control Software 62
Calibration 68
Saving the Image 75

Chapter 5: Modifying the Image 85
A Brief History of Image-Editing Software 86
Image-Editing Software Today 88
Anatomy of an Image Editing Program 92

Chapter 6: Using the Image 105
Legal Issues 105
Page Layout Programs 106
Graphical Word Processors 114
Illustration Programs 115
Presentation Programs 118
Multimedia Programs 119
Forms Programs 120

Chapter 7: Producing the Image 121

Producing Output 122
PostScript 124
Output Technologies 126

Chapter 8: Working with an Imaging Service 149

Buying Out Scans 152
Output Options 156
Selecting a Service Bureau 157
Going to Print 158
New Printing Technologies 160
Help from Your Commercial Printer 163

Chapter 9: Document Imaging 165

Optical Character Recognition 165
Document Scanners 174
Portable Documents 176
The Future of Scanning 176

Appendix: Glossary of Terms 181

Index 197

INTRODUCTION

A few years can seem like an eternity in the personal computer business, and nowhere has this been more apparent than in the market for desktop scanners. When we published the first edition of *The Scanner Book* in 1989, scanners capable of sensing 256 levels of gray were just beginning to become affordable. Color scanners were expensive and produced images of questionable quality. The most sophisticated off-the-shelf image-editing programs for the Macintosh were ImageStudio and Digital Darkroom, both of which were limited to working with gray-scale images. Image-editing programs for PC-compatible computers were even more primitive.

How times have changed! Today you can purchase a 24-bit color scanner for less than you once paid for an 8-bit gray-scale model. Sheetfed scanners have nearly disappeared, while new scanning technologies—slide and transparency scanners, drum scanners, and more—have emerged to serve the growing market for high-end color image capture. ImageStudio has gone the way of the dinosaur, while users now can choose from a wide range of powerful color image-editing programs like Adobe Photoshop, HSC Software's Live Picture, Fauve xRes, and Micrografx Picture Publisher, just to name a few.

The desktop scanner, barely an adolescent five years ago, has grown to full adulthood. But the stakes have grown as well. Just as we expect more from an adult than from a teenager, so we have placed greater demands on scanning technology. Instead of capturing images "for position only" or for reproduction as black-and-white halftones on newsprint, scanners are now used to digitize photographs for use in slick magazines and advertising brochures. Color prepress experts—so-called "dot doctors"—are quick to whip out their magnifying glasses (known in the business as "loupes") to examine the print quality of scanned images. And woe be to the scanner operator whose images turn out to be too dark or too light or otherwise unfit for publication.

In the early days of desktop publishing, typographers saw their livelihoods threatened by the dreaded combination of a computer, page layout software, and laser printer (and later the imagesetter). They scoffed at the quality of type produced on the desktop, proudly stating (while, in secret, fervently hoping) that this technology was a mere toy, that it would never threaten their craft. Today's graphic arts market is littered with the carcasses of these type experts—or at least the ones who didn't make the transition to the new technology.

A similar phenomenon has occurred with color prepress technology. At first, color prepress experts scoffed at the quality of scanned color images—and with some justification. Early desktop color scanners, at least the affordable ones, offered limited image quality, and most users had no idea of what it took to scan an image that would look acceptable when it was finally printed. But thanks to advances in hardware and software, color images produced with desktop scanners are looking better and better. Those same "dot doctors" who used to bask in the superiority of proprietary prepress systems now find themselves hard-pressed to tell the difference between an image scanned into a Macintosh or PC and one scanned on a $200,000 dedicated prepress system.

But hardware and software don't tell the whole story. We live in an Information Age where the most powerful asset is knowledge. Software developers have made great strides in automating such arcane functions as scanner calibration, but the quality of a scanned image is still largely dependent on the skill and experience of the operator. In the hands of a novice, the most sophisticated hardware and software in the world is likely to produce crud. A skillful user with access to the most basic equipment is often capable of producing remarkably good-looking images.

In 1989, we attempted to lead users through the wilderness of software functions and hardware specifications that characterize most aspects of the microcomputer market. We tried to demystify the technobabble that kept users from taking full advantage of the scanner's capabilities. Since then, users have become more sophisticated, only to find that the knowledge needed to use the technology reaches new heights.

Almost since its original publication, many readers of the first *Scanner Book* have clamored for a new edition that covers color scanning, new image-editing packages, and other advances in hardware and software. Writing and producing such a book can be a frustrating experience, because technology and products change rapidly. But the need for a road map is there, and we have tried to answer that need with this book.

As with the original *Scanner Book*, we will assume that the reader, at least at first, is new to scanning and imaging technology. To the greatest extent possible, we will try to avoid technical terminology, or at least will explain the terms as best we can as we go along. At the same time, we want to offer something of value for the more experienced user. In the early chapters, we will try to bring the newcomers up to speed, preparing them for the more advanced subject matter later in the book.

By now it should be apparent—as it was with the original *Scanner Book*—that we will devote as many pages to discussing software as we do to hardware. It is software that brings out the true power of desktop scanners, from the moment you capture the image to when you produce it on a printer or imagesetter.

The content of the book has been largely rewritten to reflect the many changes that have occurred in scanner technology over the past five years. But the structure remains pretty much the same, except for the first chapter. In the original *Scanner Book*, we began with a rather whimsical view of some real-life scanner applications. Though we haven't lost our sense of humor (at least we hope not), we figure that by now, most users probably have a pretty good idea of what scanners can do. Instead, we begin with a general introduction to imaging, with a focus on color and how it is treated on the desktop.

In Chapter Two, How Scanners Work, we'll discuss how the scanner itself operates—in non-technical language—examining the various categories of scanner hardware: flatbed, slide, drum; color or gray-scale; CCD versus PMT.

In Chapter Three, Scanning Workstations, we'll also look at other hardware considerations, such as memory and disk storage requirements; the various front-ends used with scanners; and peripheral devices like mass storage drives and 24-bit displays that will help you get the most out of your scanner.

Chapter Four, Capturing the Image, looks at various kinds of images and how they are captured and stored by your scanner control software. We discuss the importance of resolution and file size, and the various file formats like TIFF, PICT, and JPEG in which scanned images are stored. We also discuss the process of scanner calibration and new techniques like automatic picture replacement that make it much easier to handle large file sizes.

Chapter Five, Editing the Image, examines what you can do with an image once you acquire it. We provide a detailed discussion of image-editing programs like Photoshop, showing how they can be used to enhance or completely alter scanned images. Advanced techniques like masking, filtering, and color correction are also discussed.

Chapter Six, Using the Image, discusses what you can do with scanned images once they have been modified to your satisfaction. We describe several page layout programs that accept scanned input, including QuarkXPress and PageMaker, showing how you can use tools in those programs to further adjust your images. We also discuss other software packages that use scanned images, including illustration programs and forms design software.

Chapter Seven, Producing the Image, discusses the many issues involved in printing and reproducing an image. This includes use of color printers, imagesetters, and offset reproduction techniques.

In Chapter Eight, Working with an Imaging Service, we discuss the role that service bureaus and commercial printers typically play in producing output of scanned images.

Chapter Nine, Document Imaging, describes the process by which printed documents are scanned and converted to electronic documents that can be edited with a word processor. It covers the features to look for in OCR software and offers tips on using OCR as a tool for text and database files.

Finally, the Appendix presents a glossary of scanner-related terms.

CHAPTER 1

An Introduction to Digital Imaging

A scanner is a piece of hardware that converts images on paper into a format that can be used by a computer. It is a bridge between the "real world" and the digital domain of the Mac or PC. Images on paper become images on the computer screen, where they can be modified or combined with other images, and eventually printed on a laser printer, imagesetter, or other output device.

You may notice that the word "image" keeps popping up. Most of us live in a world of images: frequencies of light reflected or transmitted from external objects, into our eyes and through our optic nerves to our brains. This biological form of imaging is so integral to our lives that we usually take it for granted (unless we have a friend or relative who happens to be blind).

Computers are capable of imaging as well, but the way they handle images is much different. Most early microcomputers, in fact, could not capture or display images in any true sense. Instead, they were limited to presenting character-based information: the familiar 80-column by 25-line matrix of letters, numbers, and symbols that still characterizes many computer screens. Many people continue to rely on software packages that use the character-based display, even if their computers have graphics capabilities.

Digital imaging is the technology by which computers are used to capture, modify, and produce images. It is the first part of this process—image capture—where scanners come into play. Therefore, to understand how scanners work, it helps to have some general knowledge of digital imaging.

In this chapter, we will cover the basics of digital imaging. We will describe how computers handle information in general, which lays the groundwork for an understanding of how computers handle images.

Although computers are highly complex pieces of electronics, there is no mystery about how they perform their magic. A computer is essentially a number-cruncher, what one author once described as "an abacus on amphetamines." To a computer, an image is little more than a series of numbers.

One focus of this chapter is color imaging, an area where scanners have made major advances in recent years. When we wrote the first edition of *The Scanner Book*, desktop color scanners were expensive and offered limited functionality. Today, the vast majority of new scanners have color capability.

Bits and Bytes

Digital images fall into one of three categories: black-and-white, gray-scale, and color. In all cases, these images consist of an arrangement of dots. The dots may be too tiny to discern with the naked eye, but they are dots nonetheless. Later, we will discuss "object-oriented" images, which consist of geometric shapes rather than dots. But even object-oriented images are displayed on the monitor or printed as dots.

The scanner's function is to convert images on paper into this series of dots. Black-and-white images are the simplest: each dot is either black or white. In a gray-scale image, each dot can be one of many shades (usually limited to 256) of gray. Color images in a computer system typically include anywhere from 256 to more than 16 million colors.

Computer users sometimes refer to images as containing a certain number of "bits." A black-and-white image is "single bit." An image with 256 gray shades or colors is "8-

bit, or 2^8." A 24-bit image has about 16.7 million colors (2^{24}).

"Bit" is short for "binary digit," which is where we get the term "digital." Computers, as you probably know, handle information in the form of numbers. That's what they're good for: processing gobs and gobs of numbers at incredible speeds. What you see on the screen may look like text or pictures, but to the computer, these are representations of numbers.

Not just any numbers, however. We are used to a numbering scheme called Base 10. It is a system of ten digits, 0 through 9. When arranged in particular patterns, these digits can represent just about any number known to mathematics. But when processing data internally, computers use a different numbering scheme based on just two digits, 0 and 1. This numbering scheme is known as Base 2, or the binary system.

Just as you can express any number in Base 10, you can express numbers in Base 2 as well. You just need a greater number of digits to do it. The number 8 in Base 10, for example, is 1000 in Base 2. To see how this is so, we can try counting from one to eight in Base 10, then do the same thing in Base 2.

```
BASE 10: 0 1 2   3   4    5    6    7    8
BASE 2:  0  1  10 11 100 101 110 111 1000
```

Base 2 may seem like an inefficient way of doing things, especially for computers that are supposed to run so fast. But when you realize that computers handle information in the form of electrical impulses, it makes a lot of sense to work with binary numbers. When an impulse is off, the computer registers a zero, and when it is on, the computer registers a one.

These impulses are the "bits" that computer salespeople love to confuse you with. All information a computer handles boils down to combinations of bits—the presence or absence of electricity—arranged and rearranged with mind-numbing speed as they flow within its circuitry.

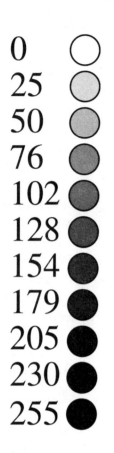

0	
25	
50	
76	
102	
128	
154	
179	
205	
230	
255	

In a gray-scale image, each dot can be one of 256 possible shades of gray.

One term often heard in conjunction with "bit" is "byte." A byte, to put it simply, is a series of eight bits: 00000001, 10000010, 10101010, and so on. Since there are 256 possible combinations of zeroes and ones in an eight-digit number, a byte can represent any one of 256 numbers or values. To compute how many values are possible for a given number of digits, simply raise 2 to the corresponding power. For example, a 6-bit number has 2^6—2 x 2 x 2 x 2 x 2 x 2—or 64 possible values. A 24-bit number—equivalent to 3 bytes—has about 16.7 million possible values.

These values can be used to represent many different kinds of information. It's like a code, where each different arrangement of zeroes and ones stands for a certain character, color, or gray shade.

A bit can represent one of two values: 0 or 1. This is why we call a black-and-white image "single-bit," because we can use 0 to represent white and 1 to represent black.

A byte, as we noted above, can represent one of 256 possible values from 00000000 to 11111111. One use of the byte is to represent characters. Each of these 256 values can stand for a single letter, number, or symbol used in the English language, with enough values left over to represent many non-English characters as well. Thus a 500-byte computer file has about 500 characters of information.

The eight bits in a byte can also be used to represent colors or shades of gray in a dot. For example, the binary number "00001111" could be used to represent a certain variety of red or a 5-percent shade of gray. If each dot in the image is represented in this eight-bit format, it can be one of 256 colors or gray shades.

In a 24-bit image, we have a much greater range of numbers that we can use to represent colors. Each dot can be one of approximately 16.7 million values, and thus 16.7 million colors ranging from the whitest white to the blackest black and nearly every color in between. It sounds like a big number, but this is the amount of information generally needed to accurately reproduce color photographs. We could theoretically have an image with 16.7 million shades of gray, but experience has shown that 256 shades is sufficient for the realistic reproduction of gray-scale images.

Remember that we are using the bit and byte measurements to represent each individual dot in an image. Depending on its size and resolution (the density of the dots), an image can contain thousands or even millions of dots. Therefore, we need other units of measurement to determine the amount of space consumed by an image. A "kilobyte," often abbreviated "K" or "Kb," is 1024 bytes. A "megabyte," abbreviated "MB," is 1024 kilobytes. Thanks to the growing power of computer hardware, some storage devices are measured in "gigabytes," or 1024 megabytes. A few companies have even introduced products that can store "terabytes"—1024 gigabytes of information. Later in this book, we will discuss mass storage devices in greater detail.

Now that we understand how computers handle information, we'll discuss how color is perceived in the real world and how it is represented within the digital domain.

Color Perception

For most of us, color is easy to take for granted. We may have to adjust the hue on our TV sets every now and then, but for the most part, we don't give much thought to the way color is perceived.

It is easy to overlook the complexity of color perception. Many factors affect how we perceive color images, including the level of surrounding light and the medium through which the image is presented. Our perception of printed images can vary depending on the paper stock and inks used on press. Our perception of images displayed on a television set or computer monitor can vary depending on the age and make of the tube.

Color is, to put it simply, light. You've probably seen the old experiments where a beam of light is passed through a prism and breaks apart into the colors of the rainbow. Each color represents different frequencies of light. When light of certain frequencies hits our eyes, we perceive it as the color corresponding to those frequencies.

In digital imaging, we are interested in two kinds of color: reflective color and transmissive color. Reflective color is what we see when we look at a non-luminous object. When we look at an orange, for example, we see light reflected back from the fruit. The surface of the fruit absorbs all colors except orange, then reflects the remaining frequencies (orange) back to the eye. If a surface absorbs all colors, it appears black. If it absorbs no colors, it appears white. Because the perceived color is based on what is removed from the light, reflective color is sometimes referred to as being "subtractive."

Transmissive color is color emitted from a luminous source. It includes color generated by a television set or computer display. Instead of seeing color as reflected from a light-absorbing surface, we see it directly transmitted from a light source. Transmissive color is sometimes known as "additive" color: when you add all the colors of the spectrum together, you get white (sort of the reverse of what happens when light passes through a prism).

To put it more simply, reflective color is the color of print, and transmissive color is the color of light. The distinction is important because digital imaging systems need to deal with both. Even though a scanned image may originate as a print, a scanner will convert it into a range of transmissive colors. Likewise, the monitor will display the image in the form of transmissive colors. But when the image is produced on an output device, it is converted back into reflective colors.

Color Models and Spaces

In elementary school art classes, you were probably taught about mixing paints. Mixing equal amounts of yellow and blue paint produced green. Mixing equal amounts of red and yellow produced orange. Blue and red together produced purple. If you threw paints of many different colors together, you probably ended up with a brownish mess.

This ability to combine two or more colors to produce a third color is the secret behind most forms of color display and reproduction, whether on a television set or printed page. Over the years, people have learned that they can produce a wide range of colors simply by combining a few basic colors. These basic colors used to produce other colors are known as "primaries."

When you were mixing paints in art class, you were using many different primary colors. But scientists have found that the number of true primary colors is quite limited. They have created several different color "models" or "spaces," each of which uses just three or four primary colors. These primaries, in turn, can be combined in varying amounts to create nearly any reproducible color.

The three color models used most often in computer systems are RGB, CYMK, and HLS.

The three principal color imaging models can each be represented as three-dimensional color "spaces."

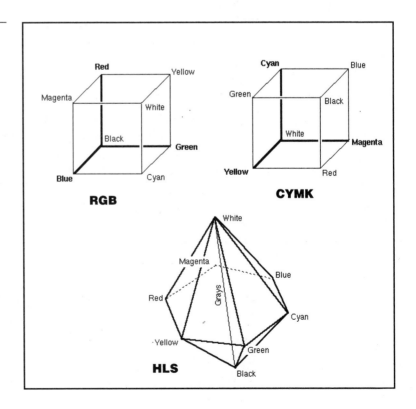

RGB

CYMK

HLS

RGB

RGB, for Red, Green, and Blue, is a model generally associated with transmissive color. Television sets, scanners, and computer displays also reproduce color using combinations of red, green, and blue. In the RGB model, colors are described as being various combinations of red, green, or blue. We noted earlier that transmissive color is additive. If you add together the maximum amounts of red, green, and blue, you get white. Remove the red, green, and blue and you get black.

CYMK

CYMK, which stands for Cyan, Yellow, Magenta, and Black, is the color model used in the printing industry. Instead of being based on the transmissive colors red, green, and blue, it is based on reflective primaries cyan (a light blue), yellow, magenta (a purplish red), and black.

This color model is sometimes known as CYM, because in theory you should be able to use cyan, yellow, and magenta to reproduce nearly any color. Unlike the transmissive RGB model, where combining all three primaries produces white, the three primaries in the CYM model theoretically combine to produce black. Likewise, if you remove all three primaries, you get white. In practice—because of the imperfections of the printing process—CYM together don't do a good job of producing black or other dark shades. This is a serious limitation, because black is usually the color of text. Therefore, the offset lithography process adds black as a fourth primary to get the best possible printing results.

HLS

HLS, for Hue, Lightness, and Saturation, is different from the other color models in that it is based on properties other than color. In the HLS model, hue refers to the actual color, lightness refers to the brightness or darkness of the color, and saturation refers to the purity of the color. Again, by balancing these three variables, you can create nearly any perceptible color.

This model is sometimes used because it is highly intuitive. Many graphics programs allow you to create your own colors by using separate software controls, such as a slider bar, to determine the level of RGB, CYMK, or HLS. As you use these controls, you can see the color produced by that combination of variables. If you did not have this ability to preview the color, you would probably be at a loss to figure out what that particular combination would produce. Imagine, for example, the color produced

Scanning Straight

APPLICATION BRIEF

There are a number of techniques you can use to make sure your image comes in straight, and not skewed, from the scanner. If your image is perfectly aligned to the edges of the sheet of paper, then it's relatively easy to align it just by sliding the page flush against the guides in your scanner. But if your artwork is skewed on the page, or if your paper isn't cut perfectly square, you'll need to find another method.

One approach is to look for horizontal or vertical line elements in the original artwork. Then, after you have done a preview scan, use the selection marquee tool to make sure that the edges of the selection rectangle align with the vertical or horizontal elements you identified in your artwork (you need not actually complete the selection; you're merely using the selection marquee as a guide).

Another technique is to scan the image as straight as you can visually, and then use your image editing software to rotate the image until it is perfectly straight. Of course, this takes some time, and it's always better to bring in clean images from the scanner than to make them clean in software.

The third, and easiest, method is to use the automatic straightening functions in scanning software such as Ofoto or PhotoFlash.

when you combine 20 percent cyan, 30 percent magenta, 40 percent yellow, and 10 percent black. You probably can't. Now imagine the color produced when you set the hue as red, the lightness at 50 percent, and the saturation at 20 percent. You might not have an exact idea of what it looks like, but you can probably come pretty close.

These models are sometimes known as "color spaces" because they can be visualized as three-dimensional objects. Each edge of the object represents one of the primary color components. In the RGB model, for example, one edge represents red, another blue, and another green. A specific color can then be represented as a point within the object.

It is important to know how color models work because electronic publishing systems must often translate the same image from one model to another. Indeed, this is one of the major challenges of producing good-looking images from the desktop. You begin with a color print that uses a CYMK model. When you scan it and display it, it becomes an RGB image. Then, when you print it, it goes back to CYMK.

Because these models are based on fundamentally different properties of light—reflective versus transmissive—there is never an exact correspondence between the image that's displayed and the image that's finally printed. An image displayed on a monitor tends to look more vibrant and more highly saturated than the same image reproduced in print. All you can hope for is a close approximation between what is scanned, what is displayed, and what is printed.

Later in this book, we will describe color management systems, which are schemes created by different manufacturers to optimize the capture, display, and output of colors in a computer systems. These color management systems depend on color spaces to ensure consistent and accurate handling of color. But more on that later.

Continuous Tones Versus Halftones

Color images are generally reproduced by one of two means: through a printing process, such as offset lithography, or by a photographic process. In the photographic process, images are exposed on a silver halide plate. In offset lithography, images are separated into four pieces of film, one each for the CYMK color components. This film is converted into plates, which are then mounted on a press (this is a bit of an oversimplification, because some printing processes involve more than the four basic primaries, but the explanation will suffice for now).

There is one key distinction between the images produced in photography and those produced in offset lithography. It is an important distinction to keep in mind later when we discuss how scanned images are produced on paper.

Photographic images are known as "continuous-tone," or "contone" for short. This means that each of the tiny particles on the film can reproduce a nearly infinite range and intensity of color. An area of red, for example, can be a relatively light, washed-out shade, an intense, highly saturated shade, or other shades in between.

In a halftone, dots of varying sizes create the impression of different levels of gray.

Printed images, that is, images reproduced through offset lithography, cannot show these continuous tones. This is a fundamental limitation of the offset printing press. When the press lays a dot of ink on the page, it cannot vary the intensity of the ink. However, it can vary the size of the dots it lays on the page.

When you look at a photograph in a newspaper, magazine, or a book like the one you're reading, what you are seeing is an optical illusion. This optical illusion has a special name: "halftone." In a halftone, dots of varying sizes are printed at a certain angle, creating what's known as a halftone "screen." In light parts of an image, the dots are relatively small, and in dark parts of an image, the dots are relatively large. All of the dots are small enough that you can barely discern them with the naked eye. Because they are so small, they create the illusion of varying tones that you see in a photograph.

In most cases, the dots are evenly spaced, so the distance between the centers of adjacent dots are the same. This distance—equivalent to the size of the largest dot— is referred to as the "screen frequency" or "line screen" of the halftone and is measured in "lines per inch" or "lpi." Relatively high screen frequencies produce sharp images that can barely be distinguished from a contone. Lower screen frequencies often give away the fact that you are looking at an optical illusion—though not enough that the illusion loses its magic.

One factor that determines screen frequency is the type of paper stock on which the image is printed. Cheap paper stocks like newsprint tend to absorb dots of ink as they are laid on the page. As the ink is absorbed, it spreads, and thus there is a limit to how small the smallest dot can be. This spreading is known as "dot gain." Costlier coated stocks used in magazines are subject to less dot gain, and thus have the potential for reproducing halftones with higher screen frequencies.

Halftones printed on newsprint in newspapers or other publications tend to have screen frequencies between 85 and 100 lines. Halftones printed in slick magazines generally range from 133 to 150 lines per inch. Coffee table books, calendars, and other high-quality printed pieces often have screen frequencies of 200 lines or more.

Later, we'll discuss a new category of screening technology called stochastic or frequency-modulated screening that uses small dots of a uniform size instead of variable-sized halftone dots. The result is an image that appears to be continuous-tone or of a high screen frequency. Stochastic screening is made possible by recent advances in imagesetter technology and thus is a new factor in graphic arts production. Again, we'll discuss this new form of screening more extensively in a later chapter.

When you scan a photograph with the intention of producing it for publication, you usually begin with a continuous-tone image that will eventually be printed as a halftone. Making this transition is one of the challenges of using scanners and imaging software to their greatest potential, and this challenge provides one of the major focuses for this book.

Electronic Publishing Systems

In the days before desktop computers became serious prepress platforms, the publishing process worked something like this:

1. A typographer working with a phototypesetting system produced galleys of type on a glossy paper. These galleys were pasted up on artboards, with blank spaces left for photographs and other images.

2. If the publication included black-and-white photographs, these were sent to a commercial printer along with the artboards and any instructions needed for resizing and cropping the images. The printer used a graphic arts camera to convert the continuous-tone images into halftones of the desired dimensions. A graphic arts camera was also used to photograph the artboards and convert them into film negatives—meaning areas to be printed in black are clear and areas without printing are black. The

printer then cut a hole in the film and taped in the halftone in a labor-intensive process known as stripping.

3. If the publication included color photographs, these were sent to a color trade shop, where they were separated into four pieces of film, each corresponding to one of the four CYMK color components. This film was then stripped in with the film containing the remainder of the publication. At the same time, a color "proof" was produced, showing the print customer how the page would look when finally printed.

4. The film was then used to create plates made of metal, plastic, or paper. In a single-color print job, just one plate was mounted on the press. In a four-color job, four plates were created and mounted. Ink in the appropriate color(s) was applied to the plates, transferred to a rubber blanket, and from there to the paper.

Electronic publishing systems using inexpensive micro-computers have revolutionized this process, making it more productive and cost-effective. Here's how the scenario above has been changed thanks to "digital prepress":

1. Photographs and other images are scanned using a desktop scanner. They are converted into the zeroes and ones—bits and bytes—described above. If necessary, the images are modified using an image-editing or color-correction program.

2. A page layout program is used to create the publication. Instead of having the text typeset into galleys and then pasted up, everything is composed on the computer screen. The scanned images are placed electronically in the page layout.

3. If the page needs to be proofed, it can be printed on one of many output devices: a laser printer for black-and-white output or one of several kinds of color printers for color output.

4. The file containing the publication is then copied to a disk. If the files are small, this can be a floppy diskette. If the files are large, it can be a removable hard disk, magneto-optical disk, or another form of removable mass storage.

Don't Limit Yourself to Two Dimensions

APPLICATION BRIEF

Remember that most flatbed scanners can sense a limited amount of depth information from objects placed on the glass. Experiment with placing coins, keys, or other three-dimensional objects on the scanner to see what happens. You may also want to try crumpling a piece of paper to see the textured effect this produces when scanned. Or try placing objects, such as bathroom tiles, linoleum, neckties, even drapery, on your scanner to pick up nifty patterns that you can reproduce.

5. The file is taken to a service bureau. There, it is produced as film on an imagesetter. If color is involved, the pages are separated as four pieces of film, each corresponding to one of the CYMK primaries. The service bureau can also use this film to produce a color proof. This proof, produced directly from the film, usually provides a more accurate idea of the final look of the printed piece than the output produced from a color printer.

6. The film is then taken to a printer, who uses it to make plates as in the example above.

There are variations on this process. In some cases, the service bureau will scan the photographs using a high-quality drum scanner—which many customers cannot afford themselves—and incorporate the images electronically into the page layout before producing film. Some service bureaus will scan the images before you design the page and return them on a disk so you can place them yourself.

New printing technologies are extending the reach of the computer to the press itself. Instead of producing film, you can send your computer output directly to the offset press. In addition, digital color copiers are sometimes used to produce limited volumes of pages as an alternative to offset lithography.

Finally, multimedia and digital video applications are creating new uses for scanned images. Instead of scanning photographs for print, some users are scanning them for use with LCD projectors, digital video productions, or interactive multimedia products on CD-ROM.

Recent advances in hardware and software have opened new vistas for the desktop scanner. But taking advantage of these opportunities—especially in color imaging—can be a tricky matter. We have already noted the challenge of converting among different color models. In addition, digital prepress systems typically include components from a variety of manufacturers, and these don't always work together as smoothly as they should. As sophisticated as the desktop tools have become, they still haven't removed all of the complexity involved in the process by which images are reproduced in print.

In the next chapter, we will begin to sort out this complexity by examining how scanners operate.

CHAPTER 2

How Scanners Work

You don't need to know how a television works to enjoy your favorite shows, and you can be the world's greatest race car driver while being completely ignorant of fuel injectors, transmissions, and the internal combustion engine. Likewise, you need not know anything about the inner workings of a desktop scanner to get good-looking images.

If you look at a scanner, you won't see much in the way of outside controls beyond the on-off switch. Some hand scanners have controls for setting brightness and contrast, but most scanning operations are performed through software supplied by the scanner manufacturer or a third-party vendor.

So you don't have to become a technical wizard to get the most from your scanner. But it does help to know some basics about how a scanner operates and how it interacts with other elements of a computer system. You need to be sure that the scanner has the proper hardware connections for your computer. You must also have sufficient memory, disk storage, and display capability to handle scanned images. Beyond this, knowing how the hardware produces images allows you to use scanner-related software to get the best possible image quality.

In this chapter, we'll look at the hardware elements of your scanner:

Its "eyes," which allow it to recognize images.

Standard hardware connections used by scanners, and what computers they work with.

The various types of scanners: flatbed, slide, transparency, drum.

And, perhaps most important of all, other hardware considerations like memory, disk storage, and screen display.

The Scanner's "Eyes"

In the last chapter, we described how computers process information—including images—in the form of digital data or bits. The basic function of a scanner is to digitize images: it converts images in the real world into a series of numbers that your computer, with the proper software, can manipulate just as it manipulates figures in a math equation. In other words, the scanner performs the function of converting analog information into digital data.

Analog information is characterized by a continuous flow, whereas digital data is characterized by discrete bits. Consider the old-style gasoline pumps you found in service stations before the Computer Age. As you held down the handle on the nozzle, a dial on the pump turned continuously, adding up the number of gallons flowing into your fuel tank. The number on the dial was directly analogous to the amount of gas pumped. With the newer digital fuel pumps, numerals are electronically displayed in fast sequence, stopping at a discrete number when you are finished. If you've pumped 10.256 gallons, the readout is the same as if you pumped 10.257 gallons.

The human visual system is sort of like an analog computer. When we view an image, what we see is reflected light of varying shades and brightness. When a scanner digitizes a photograph or other illustration, it converts light reflected from the image—analog information—into a digital format. In most cases, it measures the light by means of a photosensitive silicon chip called a charge-coupled device, or CCD.

A CCD—the "eye" of a scanner—consists of thousands of tiny elements that can measure the level of light to which they're exposed. These elements emit a weak electrical charge that corresponds to the light's intensity. In most scanners, the photosensitive elements are arranged in a single line that passes over the image, but video equipment like TV minicams use rectangular arrays.

Some drum scanners, which we will describe later, use an alternative to CCDs known as photo multiplier tubes, or PMTs. Manufacturers of PMT-based scanners claim that the PMT technology offers superior image quality, a notion that manufacturers of CCD-based scanners dispute. The truth is that both kinds of scanners can produce images of high quality. Image quality, as we will see throughout this book, depends on many factors, such as software and operator skill, that have little to do with the quality of the hardware.

Resolution

In the previous chapter, we mentioned that all digital images consist of dots. They are like small versions of the scoreboards found in most sports arenas. When an image is scanned, each CCD or PMT element "looks" at the area just above it. It then sends a signal indicating the presence of white or black, or a shade of gray in between. The signals, when processed by the computer, produce a digital image corresponding to the analog image that was scanned.

The number of photosensitive elements in a CCD determines the resolution—the density of dots—in the scanned image. If there are 2540 elements in a 8 1/2-inch linear CCD, we get 300 elements per inch or potential resolution of 300 dots per inch (dpi). An image scanned at 300 dpi will have greater detail than one scanned at a lower resolution because it is storing information about smaller pieces of the image.

It used to be that most scanners offered 300-dpi resolution. But this has changed. Many flatbed scanners now offer resolutions ranging from 600 to 1200 dpi. Slide and transparency scanners offer higher resolution, and drum scanners the highest resolution of all, as much as 5000 dpi.

Although many scanner manufacturers have improved the resolution of their scanners, you have to be careful when judging the value of this specification. Many scanners with 300- or 400-dpi CCD arrays are advertised as being 600- or 800-dpi. They do this through a process known as "interpolation."

There are two kinds of interpolation: hardware and software. In hardware interpolation, the scanning mechanism slows down as it scans the image. This has the effect of doubling the vertical resolution by causing the scanned dots to overlap. In software interpolation, the scanning software analyzes the position of each dot and makes what is essentially an educated guess about what the image would look like at the higher resolution. Some scanners use both forms of interpolation, hardware interpolation to boost the vertical resolution and software interpolation to boost the horizontal resolution.

In one sense, interpolation does increase the resolution of scanned images, because the images have twice as many dots per line than an image that has not been interpolated. But in most cases, an image that achieves 600-dpi resolution through interpolation will not be as sharp as an image that achieves that resolution with 600 elements per inch in the CCD. The latter is known as the "true" or "optical" resolution of the scanner, and is generally a better measure of the image quality the scanner can produce. Sometimes you have to read a scanner's spec sheet pretty carefully to know whether its resolution is truly 800 dpi as opposed to a 400-dpi scanner that uses interpolation.

Bit Depth

In addition to resolution, another factor that distinguishes one scanner from another is its "bit depth" or "pixel depth" ("pixel," short for "picture element," is a term that refers to the smallest unit in an electronic display; it is sometimes used as a synonym for "dot").

In the last chapter, we discussed the differences among single-bit, 8-bit, and 24-bit images. A single-bit image consists of two colors, usually black and white. An 8-bit

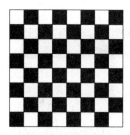

Dithered images simulate the appearance of gray values by alternating the use of black and white dots in varying proportions.

image consists of 256 colors or shades or gray. A 24-bit image consists of 16.7 million colors. "Bit depth" is a term used to describe the ability of a scanner to capture these various kinds of images.

Most early desktop scanners were limited to single-bit capability: they were good for scanning text or black-and-white line art and little else. However, some of these scanners "cheated," using a rather ingenious technique called "dithering" to simulate gray-scale capability. When scanning an area of gray, the scanner software converted the gray shade into a pattern of dots. Such dot patterns are similar to the halftones described in the last chapter.

Unfortunately, dithered images have many disadvantages. When the halftone pattern is imposed at the beginning of the scanning process, rather than during printing, the image is locked into that pattern. If you later try to enlarge or reduce the image, you will create a rather unsightly form of interference known as a "moiré pattern." A moiré, which appears like a grid on top of the picture, occurs when one screen pattern is laid on top of another. You can see this for yourself by holding two window screens together.

Dithered images also appear to be coarse because the process requires that individual dots—which would otherwise be used to add sharpness to the image—are clustered into halftone "cells," each of which is equivalent to a single dot in a gray-scale image. If a halftone cell consists of 16 dots—four on each side—you essentially reduce the resolution to one-fourth of what it would be otherwise.

Thanks to advances in scanner hardware, dithered images are pretty much a thing of the past. But some developers of scanner software still give you the option of saving images in a dithered format. In fact, some give you lots of options for creating different kinds of dither patterns, which go by names like "Bayer" or "fatting." Developers do this, no doubt, in an attempt to satisfy computer users who still have the older scanners.

Banding occurs (top) if a scanner lacks the ability to sense a sufficient number of gray levels.

The next step up from a single-bit scanner is a gray-scale scanner. A gray-scale scanner can see each dot in the image as one of many levels of gray. Early gray-scale scanners, such as the original Hewlett-Packard ScanJet or Apple Scanner, were four-bit models, limited to sensing 16 levels of gray. Unfortunately, these weren't much better than single-bit scanners, because 16 levels of gray just aren't enough to produce a realistic reproduction of an image. If you scanned an image with a rich variety of gray tones, you would see "banding" in areas of transition between one tone and another. Instead of smooth transitions, the image would consist of discrete bands corresponding to the 16 gray shades.

The real breakthrough came with 8-bit gray-scale scanners, those capable of sensing 256 levels of gray. As far as the human eye is concerned, an image with 256 gray shades is nearly indistinguishable from one with an infinite range of shades. These were the first scanners capable of producing realistic photographic images.

Color Scanners

The next breakthrough came when manufacturers began offering inexpensive color scanners. Most color scanners have 24-bit image-capture capability: the images they produce can have up to 16.7 million colors. However, these scanners really are not much different from gray-scale models. In fact, some color scanners are little more than gray-scale scanners with the addition of color filters. They have three filters, one red, one green, one blue. These filters are like pieces of tinted color film. If you remember from the last chapter, the RGB color model is one way of describing colors, especially transmissive colors. Almost any color can be reproduced, or at least approximated, as a certain combination of red, green, and blue.

When a color scanner captures an image, it does it in three passes. First it moves the red filter into place, then scans the image. It does the same with the blue and green filters. These filters separate the image into three layers, one for each of the primary colors. The scanning software then uses this information to create a single image combining the layers.

Some color scanners use a single-pass mechanism that captures all three primary colors in one sweep. Their manufacturers claim that this approach produces better-looking images because the three color components have tighter registration—that is, each color layer aligns more precisely with the other layers. But the end result is the same, and it is often difficult to tell any difference in the quality produced by a single-pass scanner and a three-pass scanner.

In addition to bit depth and resolution, color scanners are also distinguished by characteristics known as "color accuracy" and "dynamic range."

Color accuracy refers to how well the scanner reproduces colors. Many scanners, for example, have a tendency to darken midtones, that is, colors that are neither light nor dark. Some scanners have difficulty reproducing fleshtones. Others may add a reddish or greenish cast to the image. These problems can usually be corrected through color calibration, which we will discuss in the next chapter.

Dynamic range refers to the ability of the scanner to distinguish among slight variations in gray or color shades in an image. In theory, a 24-bit scanner can identify 256 shades each of red, green, or blue, for a total of 16.7 million possible colors. In practice, due to "noise" that interferes with the scanning process, that same scanner may be recognizing somewhat less than 256 shades of each primary color. The result can be an image in which tones do not blend smoothly into one another.

Some scanners compensate for this by offering bit depths that exceed 8 bits per color. Instead, they may scan at 10 or 12 bits per pixel (per color), for a total of 30 or 36 bits per pixel of image data. The scanning software then uses this additional information to produce a 24-bit image. The final image has the same amount of data as one produced by a 24-bit scanner, but with smoother color transitions.

Gray-scale scanners are also distinguished by their accuracy and dynamic range, but these characteristics are not quite as important with gray-scale images because we tend to be more forgiving of imperfections in black-and-white halftones, especially when it comes to dynamic range. Just as calibration functions can correct problems in color scanning accuracy, they can also compensate for scanning inaccuracies with gray-scale images.

Scanning Mechanisms

While all scanners perform similar operations, they can vary widely in appearance. One key distinction is the means by which the device handles pages and other image sources. Hand-held scanners require that the user manually guide a scanning head over an image. Flatbed scanners use a flat glass platen on which the image is placed. Drum scanners use a cylindrical drum to which the image is affixed.

It would seem that the method by which you insert an image into the scanning mechanism would have little bearing on image quality. But certain types of mechanisms are usually associated with certain levels of scanning quality, with hand scanners on the bottom, flatbed scanners in the middle, and drum scanners on top. However, some manufacturers offer high-priced flatbed scanners that rival the quality of drum scanners.

Hand scanners are inexpensive tools that work with small originals.

Hand-Held Scanners

Hand scanners have become the poor cousins of the scanner market. Though inexpensive, they are not considered serious options for quality imaging work.

Gang Scan Small Originals

APPLICATION BRIEF *Sometimes when you are scanning a large number of small images such as wallet-sized portraits, you can save yourself time by placing several images on the glass simultaneously, rather than one at a time. Even if your scanning software doesn't support gang scanning, you can scan all the images together if they all use roughly the same scanning parameters. You can then use the crop and cut functions of your image-editing software to break the large image into individual images. If you find that the images have different brightness or contrast settings, you can still save time be leaving them in position on the glass and then capturing each image separately.*

Hand scanners are operated by manually running a scanning head over an image. Small rollers on the bottom of the scanning head serve to guide the hand. This is one limitation of the hand scanner, because the human hand is often unsteady, adding to the possibility that the image will be distorted. Some manufacturers offer plastic guides for hand scanners to ensure a steadier, straighter course for the hand to follow. You place the guide over the page to be scanned, then place the scanner within the gap in the middle of the guide. The edges of the guide prevent your hand from wavering.

In addition to their reliance on the human hand, most hand scanners are limited to a narrow scanning area ranging from two-and-a-half to five inches in width. Again, some software developers have come up with workarounds for this limitation. Through a function called "stitching," they allow you to scan an image in separate swaths. You can then combine these swaths into a single image using the stitching function in the software.

Another problem with hand scanners is that many are limited in the number of colors or gray shades they can recognize. This is not universally true, however: some hand scanners can capture 8-bit gray-scale or even 24-bit color.

Hand scanners do have their uses. They are great for digitizing logos or other small artwork, especially in black-and-white. They can also be used in combination with certain optical character recognition programs (see Chapter Nine) for capturing text.

The big advantage of hand scanners is their low cost. This was especially true a few years ago, when most flatbed scanners were priced at $2000 or more. But prices for flatbed scanners have fallen much more rapidly than prices for hand scanners, and as a result, the difference can amount to just a few hundred dollars. Because flatbed scanners offer much more functionality, the savings made possible by hand scanners are not so appealing any more.

Sheetfed Scanners

Sheetfed scanners, also known as edge-fed scanners, are the dinosaurs of the scanner market. A few years ago, they occupied a middle portion of the scanner market between flatbed scanners and hand scanners. But as prices for flatbed scanners have fallen, the market for sheetfed scanners has nearly disappeared.

In one sense, however, sheetfed scanners are the most popular scanners on the planet, and you probably have one in your office. It's found in your fax machine, which is essentially a sheetfed scanner combined with a high-speed modem and thermal or plain-paper printer. As you can see when you send a page over the fax, it uses a roller mechanism to pull the paper past a stationary scanning element.

Sheetfed scanners are great when they are part of a fax machine. After all, we usually don't rely on a fax machine to produce images of high quality. But in the arena of electronic publishing, sheetfed scanners have many disadvantages over flatbed models. The scanner's roller mechanism, while more precise than the human hand, does not allow for the precise alignment made possible by flatbed scanners. Sheetfed scanners are also limited to working with standard-sized sheets of paper.

A handful of companies continue to manufacture sheetfed scanners, but they have ceased to be a factor in the electronic imaging market.

Flatbed Scanners

Flatbed scanners, which resemble desktop photocopiers, use a glass platen on which pages are laid flat and covered with a lid.

Flatbed scanners probably represent the largest segment of the scanner market, at least in terms of dollar sales if not number of units sold. Most models sold these days offer a minimum resolution of 300-dpi, with 400- and 600-dpi models increasingly available. Most also offer 8-bit gray-scale and 24-bit color capability, though some of the less expensive models are limited to gray-scale image capture. Most offer a letter- or legal-sized scanning area, though a few tabloid-format flatbeds are available.

Flatbed scanners have many advantages over hand-held and sheetfed scanners. They can accommodate odd-sized originals that aren't easily handled by sheetfed scanners, and large-sized images that exceed the dimensions of hand-held scanners. You can easily perform "preview" scans, where the software scans the image at low resolution and presents it in a window on the screen, allowing you to determine which portion of the image you want to use for your final scan.

Flatbed scanners resemble desktop photocopiers. The image to be scanned is placed on a platen under the lid.

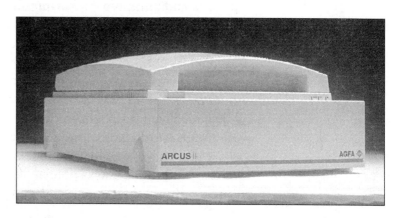

Some manufacturers offer transparency options for their flatbed scanners. Without these transparency options, flatbeds are limited to working with reflective copy only. With such an option, you can scan 35mm slides or larger-format transparencies.

These transparency options are mechanisms that shine a bright, consistent light from the back of the transparency as it is being scanned. However, the results are generally inferior to what you can produce with a dedicated slide or transparency scanner, especially when scanning 35mm slides. Part of the problem is resolution: Slide scanners typically offer resolution ranging from the equivalent of 1000 dpi to 5000 dpi. Another problem is optics: the optical system in a slide scanner is designed specifically for scanning slides, while most flatbed scanners are designed with reflective copy in mind.

If you have a small light table, you can jury-rig your own inexpensive transparency option by turning it upside-down and placing it on top of the slide or transparency as it is being scanned. However, don't expect great-looking results.

Another option sometimes offered by manufacturers is an automatic document feeder, which allows you to stack a series of pages that are automatically fed into the scanner. This option is primarily used in optical character recognition (OCR) applications, which are discussed in Chapter Nine.

Most flatbed scanners are not considered suitable for high-end color prepress work for many of the same reasons they are not generally used for scanning slides and transparencies. However, there is nothing inherent in the flatbed mechanism that causes such limitations. Most manufacturers are aiming their flatbeds at a certain segment of the imaging market, one that is somewhat price-sensitive and doesn't require the precision of high-end slide and drum scanners. A few companies, such as Scitex and Linotype-Hell, manufacture flatbeds that are designed to compete with drum scanners at the high end of the market.

Slide Scanners

Slide scanners are designed specifically for capturing images on 35mm slides. Slides are popular media for storing images because they are compact while generally offering better photographic reproduction than prints. They are also better suited to transmitting information into the scanner.

With most slide scanners, the slide is inserted directly into a slot in the scanner, or placed in a holder that is then inserted into the scanning mechanism. Because these scanners are so specialized, they cannot be used with prints or large-format transparencies.

Most slide scanners are standalone units that sit next to the computer. However, some manufacturers offer slide scanners that can be installed in an empty disk drive bay in the computer, thus saving disk space. One danger in this kind of design is that heat generated by the computer (and the scanner itself) can affect the quality of the scan. For this reason, internally mounted slide scanners tend to be less costly models used in applications where color quality is not absolutely critical.

In addition to scanning slides, many slide scanners can also be used to scan 35mm negatives used to create prints. However, the scanning software must be capable of converting the negative image into a positive. In theory, you can perform this conversion with an image-editing program, but this is not as easy as it may seem. Simply reversing the color values (a process we'll describe in Chapter Five) usually produces images in which the colors are distorted.

Slide scanners generally offer resolution ranging from about 1000 to 5000 dpi. The least expensive models capture images at 24 bits per pixel. However, some offer as much as 48-bit-per-pixel image capture. The final image may not have this much data, but the scanner uses the higher setting to account for noise. The scanning software looks at the image and essentially boils it down to the most accurate 24 bits of color data.

Transparency scanners can accommodate 35mm slides or 4x5 film transparencies.

Transparency Scanners

Transparency scanners are similar to slide scanners, except they can accommodate transparencies up to 4x5 inches in addition to 35mm slides. Some use a scanning mechanism similar to a small flatbed, with a platen containing holders in which the transparencies are placed. Others use detachable holders for the slide or transparency. Some transparency scanners allow for "gang scanning" of 35mm slides. Because of the larger image area, you can place several 35mm slides in the holder.

Transparency scanners are more flexible than slide scanners, but are also much more expensive. They are sometimes used for producing images used in print advertising or packaging—images that are often submitted in the form of larger transparencies.

Drum Scanners

Drum scanners, derived from the scanners used in proprietary color systems, are used for the most demanding prepress applications, where quality image reproduction is an absolute requirement. They are also used in situations where an image must be enlarged to many times its original size with minimal loss of quality. Drum scanners typically offer the highest levels of resolution, ranging up to 5000 dpi.

True to their name, drum scanners use a transparent drum to which the image to be scanned is affixed. The image can be a print or transparency. The drum is placed

Drum scanners offer resolution ranging up to 5000 dpi.

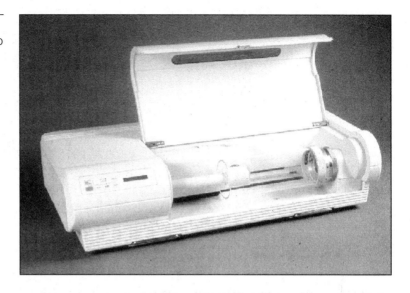

in a cavity within the scanner, which is covered with a lid. The size of the drum determines the maximum size of the image that can be scanned. Some drum scanners use PMT light sensors, while others use CCDs.

Some color separation houses have large, expensive drum scanners that are part of proprietary prepress systems. These systems include links that allow transfer of the images to Macintosh or PC media. Some manufacturers have developed interface products that allow you to connect one of these proprietary scanners directly to a microcomputer, but these tend to be expensive in their own right. Desktop drum scanners, on the other hand, are designed specifically for use with a Mac or PC. They tend to be more compact than proprietary drum scanners, but offer similar quality.

Drum scanners offer the highest level of image quality and the greatest flexibility, because they can handle slides, transparencies, and reflective media. But these advantages don't come cheaply; most desktop drum scanners are priced at $40,000 to $50,000 or even more. As noted above, several manufacturers offer high-end flatbed scanners designed to compete with drum units. These scanners can match the image quality of drum models, but are also as costly as their cylindrical competitors.

Other Scanners

Flatbed, slide, and drum don't necessarily tell the whole story when it comes to scanning mechanisms. A few scanners use camera-like mechanisms that include CCDs. The advantage is that you can scan three-dimensional objects in addition to flat images. However, the new generation of digital cameras offer the same benefit with the added convenience of portability.

A few early, primitive scanners were scanning heads that you mounted on the printhead of a dot-matrix printer. They were inexpensive, but also slow and difficult to work with. The availability of hand scanners—not to mention declining prices and improved quality in flatbed scanning technology—made these products obsolete.

Alternatives to Scanners

Scanners are not the only means by which images can be digitized. Video boards, sometimes known as frame-grabbers or digitizers, can convert analog video signals from a camera, VCR, or other source into a digital format. Digital cameras from companies like Leaf, Kodak, and Dicomed can capture images directly in digital format and then transmit them into the computer system without the need for a video board. Some of these cameras are self-contained units that include optics, CCDs, and some method for storing images. Others—typically more costly models—are camera backs that attach to standard 35mm or portrait cameras.

One difference between scanners and these camera-based forms of image-capture is the way they handle resolution. Scanners measure resolution in terms of dots per inch. Digital cameras and video frame-grabbers measure resolution in terms of total pixels, such as 680 by 480. No matter how large the photographed object, the image will always measure 680 dots in the horizontal direction and 480 vertically.

Digital cameras can capture photographs directly in digital form.

Another difference is that scanners can capture images from film or paper while digital cameras capture images

HOW SCANNERS WORK

directly from the real world. You can thus take a shot and load the image into your computer without the need for photo processing or scanning. This can save time and money, especially if image quality is paramount. However, in most cases, you still get better quality by shooting photographs to film and then using a scanner to digitize the images.

Digital cameras cover a wide range of price and performance, from under-$1000 models with relatively limited resolution to units priced at $20,000 or more that can offer a high level of image quality. Some of the more costly units are limited to capturing still objects because of lengthy exposure times. One popular application for these cameras is product photography for catalog work.

Another alternative to the scanner is a technology from Eastman Kodak known as Photo CD. With Photo CD, your photofinisher can process a roll of film and place the images in digital form on a compact disc. Images on the disc can then be read into a computer system equipped with a CD-ROM drive. The system used to create Photo CDs includes a high-quality scanner along with automatic color correction software.

Eastman Kodak's Photo CD Imaging Workstation includes a high-speed film scanner and a CD writer.

Clean Your Glass Regularly

APPLICATION BRIEF

Remember that the glass surface on your flatbed scanner is just like a window on your artwork. If the glass isn't clean, you may be introducing unwanted specs or other noise into your scanned image. Use a standard glass cleaner and a soft, lintless cloth to clean the glass. Spray the cleaner on the cloth first and then wipe the glass.

Considering the low cost of a CD-ROM drive, Photo CD offers a cost-effective way to bring quality images into your computer system. How well these images compare with scanned images is open to debate, and obviously depends on the kind of scanner you are comparing them to.

Kodak offers various flavors of Photo CD, including a "Pro" format for professional photographers, capable of storing large-format transparencies, and a "Print" format intended for prepress applications.

Photo CD is a broad subject deserving of an entire book in its own right. In fact there is such a book, *Photo CD: Quality Photos at Your Fingertips*, by electronic photography expert John Larish. If you want to learn more about Photo CD, we recommend that you read that book.

CHAPTER 3

Scanning Workstations

The scanner, of course, is but one component in a computer system. If you want to get the most from your scanner, you need to use it with hardware sufficiently powerful to display, manipulate, and produce output from scanned images.

In this chapter, we'll look at the various pieces of a computer system used for color scanning applications.

Host Computer

The most important consideration is the computer with which you use your scanner. For the most part, this is probably one of several models of Apple's Macintosh series or a PC-compatible with a 386, 486, or Pentium chip. Unix workstations from companies like Sun Microsystems, Silicon Graphics, and others are also used with scanners.

Macintosh

The Macintosh was the first inexpensive computer system developed with graphics applications in mind. It was the Macintosh that established the application category known as desktop publishing. Because of the Mac's graphics capabilities and its trendsetting position in the graphics market, it remains the most popular hardware platform among designers, ad agencies, magazine publishers, and graphics professionals.

When the Macintosh was first introduced in 1984, it featured several innovations that created a revolution in the personal computer market. It was the first popular computer with its own graphical user interface (GUI). Instead of the 80-column by 25-line character-based display of IBM PC-compatibles, it featured a bit-mapped display in which each dot on the screen could be turned on or off. This meant that in addition to displaying text, the Mac could also display pictures.

The Mac also introduced a new way of interacting with the user. Instead of requiring the user to memorize a series of English-like commands for copying, moving, and deleting files, it presented an on-screen representation of a desktop. Each file was represented by a small picture known as an "icon." Directories—storage locations for groups of files—were represented as folders. When you opened a folder, all the files contained within were shown in a window-like frame.

Integral to the GUI is a hardware device called a "mouse." The original mice were small hand-held units, connected to the computer, with rollers on the bottom and a button on top. Since the introduction of the original mice, manufacturers have introduced alternatives like trackballs—essentially an upside-down mouse—and digitizer tablets, which use pen-like styli or mouse-like units called cursors.

The GUI—actually invented at a Xerox Corporation facility known as the Palo Alto Research Center—revolutionized the personal computer business. At the time, the big complaint about PCs was their "user-unfriendliness." They were difficult to use and required you to memorize a series of sometimes cryptic commands. The GUI was designed to be much more "intuitive," in other words, to better reflect the way users actually thought and worked.

The side benefit of the GUI is that it enabled microcomputers to perform graphics applications. But early Macs were woefully underpowered as graphics machines, with limited memory, speed, disk storage, and display capabilities. Over the years, however, the Macintosh has evolved into a powerful platform for graphics applications. The machine is available in many varieties, from inexpensive Macintosh Classics to the Macintosh Quadra and new PowerPC machines. These models are differentiated by their display capabilities, expansion options, speed, memory, and disk storage.

One important consideration in any desktop computer system is the microprocessor that represents the "brain" of the machine. The microprocessor in the Macintosh is made by Motorola. The first Macs used a Motorola 68000, whose successors include the 68020 (in the original Mac II), 68030 (Mac SE/30, IIcx), and 68040 (Quadra). The newest chip from Motorola is the PowerPC, which uses a powerful kind of hardware "architecture" known as RISC, short for reduced-instruction set computing. Explaining the RISC architecture is beyond the scope of this book, but suffice it to say that RISC chips are extremely powerful when performing graphics functions.

The rule of thumb when working with scanners—and graphics applications in general—is that more is better. You can never have enough memory or disk storage, and you can never have a processor that is too fast. The more powerful your computer, the better off you'll be when working with scanned images.

PC Compatibles

The original IBM PC was never intended as a graphics computer, and even its successors were seriously limited in their ability to handle graphics. However, thanks to a number of developments, PC compatibles have made tremendous strides in recent years, and can perform most, if not all, of the graphics functions that a Macintosh can perform. Most scanners are now offered in Macintosh and PC versions, and most of the leading graphics packages run on both kinds of computers.

PCs were originally manufactured by IBM, but the vast majority of PC-compatible computers are now offered by other companies. These PC compatibles were once known as "clones" because they mimicked the original PC. But the term has dropped from usage because it implies that the compatibles are somehow inferior to the "real thing"—

which IBM itself ceased manufacturing when it introduced its PS/2.

The common denominator among PC compatibles is a chip made by Intel. The original PCs used Intel 8088 and 8086 chips. The 8088/8086 begat the 80286, which begat the 80386.

The 386, as it came to be called, was a breakthrough chip that made it possible to build powerful graphics-capable computers. Its advantages were speed, a wider "bus" (sort of a superhighway for moving data), and the capability to address a large amount of memory. This memory-addressing capability is crucial when working with scanned images, because they tend to require a large amount of RAM (more on that below).

The 386 begat a still more-powerful chip called the 486. Both chips come in several varieties with differing "clock speeds" determining the rate at which data is processed. This speed is measured in megahertz (MHz). Some 386 and 486 chips are also identified with an "SX" modifier. A 386SX or 486SX are slightly less powerful versions of the basic chip.

The successor to the 486 is a new Intel chip known as the Pentium. The Pentium is a 64-bit chip, meaning that it can handle 32 times as much data as 32-bit chips like the 386 and 486. It does not use RISC technology, but it is Intel's answer to the PowerPC (though Intel would just as likely say that the PowerPC is Motorola's answer to the Pentium). However you look at it, these chips herald a new era of powerful graphics applications.

Powerful microprocessors like the 386, 486, and Pentium have done much to advance the PC as a graphics platform. But the real breakthrough for the PC came with the introduction of an "operating environment" known as Microsoft Windows.

PCs run under an operating system, also developed by Microsoft, known as DOS. An operating system is a piece of software that sits between the computer and the software applications that run on it. It is responsible for sending data to the screen and for interacting with disk drives and other peripheral devices. The operating system also handles such tasks as copying and deleting files or calling up directories of files stored on a hard disk.

In the Macintosh, the operating system is hidden from the user by means of the Mac's graphical user interface. Early users of DOS were not so fortunate. DOS was invented in the days when character-based interfaces were the norm. To copy files or perform other file management tasks, you had to learn a series of English-like commands that you entered from a prompt on the screen. Because it used a character-based interface, DOS was never intended for graphics applications.

Windows changed all this by creating a Macintosh-like user interface than ran on top of DOS, essentially hiding the underlying operating system from the user. Early versions of Windows were slow, but the environment came into its own with the introduction of Windows 3.0 in 1991. Windows is fast becoming the operating platform of choice in the PC market. Many of the most popular graphics applications for the Macintosh have been converted to run under Windows, and Windows has also providing a breeding ground for powerful graphics programs in its own right.

Computer products never stand still, and Apple and Microsoft are constantly evolving the operating systems and GUIs that run on Macs and PCs. Microsoft has introduced a new system called Windows NT (for New Technology) that goes far beyond the capability of Windows. Instead of running on top of DOS, Windows NT is a complete operating system in its own right. However, many graphics users will find that Windows 3.1, or its successor, known as "Windows 95," will be sufficient for their needs.

Many Macintosh users contend that Windows-based PCs are still no match for the Mac, and in a sense they are right. Windows has taken enormous strides in making PCs easier to use, but the Mac still has some advantages in key areas. Apple requires all hardware and software developers who create products for the Mac to adhere to strict standards for making their components work within the system. The PC is still something of a free-for-all, and getting all the components to talk to each other can be a challenge. One consequence is that some service bureaus have avoided working with Windows-based customers because of problems they've encountered producing files. However, many other service bureaus welcome Windows users with open arms.

There is little you can do with a Mac that you cannot do with a PC. But sometimes it takes a little more knowledge and a lot more patience to get the PC to work the way it should. We'll discuss some of these challenges in greater detail later in this chapter.

Unix

Though not nearly as popular as the Macintosh or PC, Unix-based workstations are also used in many graphics applications because of their enhanced processing power.

Unix is an operating system originally developed by AT&T. It was one of the first operating systems to offer multi-user and multi-tasking capabilities. Multi-user means that multiple users can run applications from the same computer. Multi-tasking means that the computer can perform multiple tasks simultaneously.

Unix-based computers tend to be very powerful, capable of handling large amounts of data at high speeds. Many run on chips using the same RISC technology found in the PowerPC. Unix is also known for its portability, meaning it can run on a wide variety of microprocessors, including those from Intel and Motorola. However, the Unix operating system is extremely user-hostile, and operators of early Unix workstations required extensive training just to handle simple operating system tasks like copying files or calling up directories of files. Another problem is that Unix comes in several varieties that are incompatible with one another.

To address these problems, companies that make Unix workstations have developed graphical user interfaces that sit on top of Unix, just as Windows sits on top of DOS. These interfaces go by names like OpenLook, NextStep, and Motif. Just as developers can create software packages that run under Windows or the Macintosh, some also offer packages for these Unix-based GUIs.

Leading manufacturers of graphically oriented Unix workstations include Sun Microsystems and Silicon Graphics. These typically are expensive pieces of equipment, but they are popular in environments where users must handle very large images that require a lot of computer power. Silicon Graphics workstations, for example, have been used to create special effects for such films as "Terminator 2" and "Jurassic Park."

The PowerPC and Pentium were designed to bring Unix-like processing power to the Mac and PC. In fact, both chips can be used to run Unix applications.

Hardware Interfaces

Another important consideration is the hardware interface—the means by which the scanner sends data to the computer system. Although the Macintosh had a head start as a platform for graphics applications, early desktop scanners had a bias toward the PC when it came to their interfaces.

In general, a PC can have one of three kinds of interfaces: serial, parallel, or proprietary. In a serial interface, bits are sent one at a time. In a parallel interface, bits are sent eight at a time. Parallel interfaces are the most popular interface for printers, while serial interfaces are typically used with modems, mice, and some printers. However, neither interface is fast enough to handle the large amounts of data transmitted by scanners. Therefore, most early scanner manufacturers sold their scanners with proprietary interfaces. These were boards that you added to a free expansion slot in the PC, designed for fast transmission of image data into the computer system.

SCSI

In the Macintosh world, peripheral devices like scanners and disk drives are connected to the computer through a high-speed interface known as SCSI (pronounced SCUH-zee), which is short for Small Computer Systems Interface. The beauty of the SCSI interface is that many peripheral devices, including scanners, can be connected to the computer through a single SCSI port. This is done by chaining the devices together with a SCSI cable. Each device in the SCSI chain is identified by a unique number from one to eight.

To save on manufacturing costs, most scanner manufacturers make one version of their scanner for both Macintosh and PC. Most early scanners, however, included a direct interface to their PC board. To connect their scanners to a Macintosh, you had to use a SCSI interface box that sat next to the scanner. The scanner was connected to the interface box, which then functioned as a device on the SCSI chain. In addition to requiring extra desk space (and an extra power cord), these SCSI boxes added to the cost of Macintosh scanners.

Manufacturers have gotten smarter, and most now offer built-in SCSI interfaces for their scanners. This means that you can connect the scanner directly to the Macintosh. For PC users, the manufacturers offer a SCSI interface board that goes into an expansion slot in the computer. PC users are no worse off, because they install an interface board just as they did before.

Despite the benefits of Windows, the hardware interface remains one area where the Macintosh has an advantage over the PC. Connecting SCSI devices to the Macintosh is a simple matter. You need to be sure that each device has a unique SCSI ID—usually determined by a setting on the scanner—and that the last device in the chain has a special kind of adapter known as a terminator. You don't even need to open the computer, since the SCSI cable plugs directly into a built-in port in the Mac.

Expansion Boards

The PC is another matter entirely. To install an interface board—either a SCSI board or a proprietary interface—you need to remove the computer casing, locate an open slot, and carefully install the board. Even small amounts of static electricity can damage the board, so you need to be sure you are insulated by wearing rubber-soled shoes or, better, a wrist strap that grounds the electricity. In theory, the board should fit comfortably in the slot, but in practice, you may find that it takes a great deal of coaxing to get the board to fit, especially if the neighboring slots are occupied.

Then there's that unique PC pecadillo known as the "address conflict." Within the computer system, data is transferred through an electronic highway known as a "bus." To communicate with scanners and other devices connected by means of expansion boards, each device must have its own unique address. However, unlike the Macintosh, the PC does not allow you to pick a simple number from one to eight. Instead, you usually need to set "dip switches"—tiny switches on the board itself—to set the correct address, which is also known (for some strange reason) an as "interrupt." If two expansion boards have the same address, you get an address conflict and neither one will work.

Each expansion board is set at the factory with a default address. If your system includes a basic set of peripherals, such as a mouse or printer, the default address will probably work without a problem. However, if you have installed a CD-ROM drive or other peripherals that require an expansion board, the possibility grows that you will run into an address conflict. In this case, you need to reset the dip switches and try again.

Your scanner manual should help you figure out which address setting to use. If you compare this ahead of time to the address settings for the other expansion boards, you should be okay. However, if you don't know what the other address settings are, it may take some trial and error to get the scanner to work properly.

Memory Requirements

Another important hardware consideration when working with scanners is memory, specifically random-access memory, or RAM. One way to conceptualize memory is to think of it as a workspace for the computer's processor. As you run an application, software and data—including image data—are copied from the disk into RAM, where they can interact under the direction of the microprocessor. The "random access" in the abbreviation means the processor can access anything in RAM at tremendous speed. Programs and data in RAM can thus be accessed at a much faster rate than programs and data stored on a hard disk. RAM is also characterized by its volatility, meaning that any data contained in RAM is lost when the computer is turned off.

When it comes to working with scanned images, the more RAM, the better. Scanned images, especially color images, consume a large amount of data. In addition, the programs that manipulate scanned images tend to be quite complex. When you have a large amount of RAM, your computer system can handle large chunks of data and software at much faster speeds than it could with a small amount of RAM.

To visualize why this is so, think of your computer system as a desk. The top of the desk represents RAM, while the drawers represent disk storage. If you have a large desktop, you can take lots of items out of the drawers and put them on the desk at the same time. You can use different tools (software) to perform various tasks with the pieces of paper (data) on the desk. With a smaller desktop, you must constantly shuffle your tools and papers from the drawers to the desktop and back again.

Some Macintosh users—especially those who work with large color images—have as much as 256 megabytes of RAM in their systems. Others can get by with eight to 16 megabytes if they are working with files of a relatively modest size. PCs running Windows require a minimum of two, and preferably four, megabytes of RAM. However, eight to 16 megabytes are still recommended if you want to work with scanned images.

One rule of thumb is to install about three times as much RAM as the largest images you plan to work with. In other words, if you plan to work with 2-megabyte images, you can get by with six megabytes of RAM. But if you want to work with 20-megabyte images, you'll need about 60 megabytes of RAM to work in an efficient manner. Of course, if you install more RAM—say five times the largest image file size—you'll work even more productively.

The nice thing about extra RAM is that it comes in handy even when you are not working with scanned images. For example, the Macintosh and Windows both allow you to run multiple programs simultaneously. The more RAM you have, the more programs you can run. Extra RAM generally speeds up most computer applications. In many cases, you will get a bigger boost from adding RAM than you will from upgrading to a faster chip.

Graphics Displays

Another important consideration when working with scanned images is the display. Just as scanners come in various bit-depths, so do displays. Some offer 8-bit gray-scale or color display, meaning they can show 256 gray shades or colors. This is sufficient if you are working with gray-scale images. However, if you want to work with photographic images, you need a 24- or 32-bit display. Otherwise, the image will be dithered: instead of showing the true colors in the image, the software will simulate those colors using the closest matches.

A display system has two essential components: the monitor and the display adapter. The monitor is basically a high-resolution color television without the tuner or sound (in fact, many color computer displays are based on the Sony Trinitron). The adapter is usually a board installed in the Mac or PC. However, some Macintosh models feature a built-in color display adapter.

The display capabilities in your system generally have more to do with the adapter than the monitor. The same monitor that shows 256 colors when connected to an 8-bit adapter will show 16.7 million colors when connected to a 24-bit adapter. Fortunately, 24-bit display adapters have come down considerably in price in recent years, especially in the PC market.

The adapter also determines the speed at which data is written to the screen along with the maximum resolution of images that can be displayed. Your basic 12- to 14-inch PC display has a maximum resolution of 640 x 480 pixels. However, larger 20- to 24-inch monitors may require a maximum resolution of 1024 x 768 or more. These large-screen monitors are popular among electronic publishing users because they can show a full page, or two pages side-by-side, without the need to scroll around the screen. However, large-screen monitors are expensive.

Some display adapters include "graphics accelerators," a chip or a separate board that increases the rate at which data is sent to the screen. Again, color images represent a large amount of data, and this data takes time to transmit through the computer system. Accelerators are especially useful with large-screen, 24-bit displays. Simple math will show you why: multiply 1024 by 768 and you get 786,432 pixels in the screen. Multiply this by 24 bits (three bytes) and you get 2,359,296 bytes, equivalent to about 2.25 megabytes. Then consider that the system is sending 2.25 megabytes of data to the screen at 60 to 80 times per second, and you can see why graphics accelerators are important.

Some color monitors also include a calibration system. This ensures that the monitor is displaying colors as

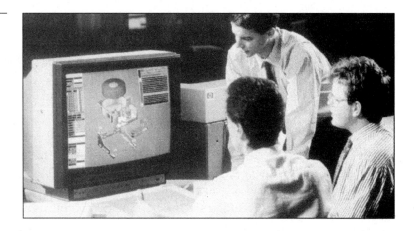

Large-screen color displays are useful components of an imaging system.

accurately as possible. A hardware calibration system includes a sensing device that you attach to the monitor. You then run calibration software, which displays a series of color images that are read by the sensor. As the sensor reads these colors, the software compares them with reference colors—in other words, the colors the monitor should be showing. The calibration device then modifies the color display to match the reference colors as closely as possible.

It is important to keep in mind that a monitor will never display a scanned image exactly as it will look in print. Printed images use reflective colors, while a displayed image uses transmissive colors. In addition, the monitor uses an RGB color model while most printed images are composed of CYMK colors. The practical consequence of this is that images look much more vibrant and colorful on the screen than they will in print. On the other hand, if you plan to use your images in a slide presentation, the display will more closely approximately what your audience will see in the slide show.

Mass Storage

One final hardware consideration is your mass storage device. As color imaging has moved to the desktop, mass storage requirements have grown almost geometrically. Six years ago, in the first edition of this book, we noted that a 40- or 80-megabyte hard disk is required for storing scanned images. Ha! Today, you will find yourself quickly filling up a 100-megabyte hard drive. Hard drives of 200 or 300 megabytes are common, and many electronic publishing systems include hard drives capable of storing a gigabyte or more.

Scanned images are not solely to blame for this explosion in storage requirements. Operating systems and graphics software also require a great deal of storage. It is not uncommon for a single graphics program to consume 10 megabytes of space by itself, not to mention the space required for the files it creates. Fortunately, prices for storage have dropped about as fast as the storage requirements have risen.

Graphics applications have also given rise to new forms of mass storage. These include disk arrays, CD-ROM drives, removable hard disks, magneto-optical drives, and shuttles.

Arrays

A disk array is essentially a collection of hard drives that work in tandem. Data is stored on multiple disks, but the computer sees the system essentially as one gigantic hard drive. The technical term for these systems is RAID, which stands for Redundant Array of Inexpensive Disks.

The technology offers several advantages, including speed and extremely large storage capacities. The speed advantage comes from the ability to perform read and write operations concurrently. In other words, a file can be stored on two separate drives with two heads working at the same time.

The capabilities of a RAID system are defined by numbers ranging from 0 to 5. For example, RAID 0 offers the concurrent read-write capability described above. RAID 1, also known as mirroring, stores identical data on two or more disks, providing automatic backup. RAID 5 provides complete fault tolerance; if one drive fails, data is automatically recovered without shutting down the system.

CD-ROM

CD-ROM drives can read data from compact discs that have been designed for use with a computer system. A CD-ROM disc, while about the same size as a diskette, can hold about 640 megabytes. However, it is a read-only medium (ROM stands for "Read-Only Memory"), meaning you can import images and other data from a CD-ROM, but you cannot write to one. Because CD-ROM discs can hold so much data, they have become popular distribution media for stock photos, fonts, multimedia titles, and especially large software packages. Kodak's Photo CD is a specially formatted CD-ROM disc.

A variation of the CD-ROM disc is the CD-R disc. Using a CD writer device, you can store data on a CD-R disc, which can then be read with a standard CD-ROM drive. Once data is stored on the CD, it cannot be deleted or written over. Using a scanner in combination with a CD writer, you can create what are essentially CD-ROM discs containing archives of scanned images.

Removable Hard Disks

Removable hard disks are similar to regular hard disks, except that you can remove the disk from the unit. This makes them handy for transporting large image or publication files—files that won't fit on a standard diskette—from one location to another. Removable hard disks are especially popular among customers of service bureaus and commercial printing companies that have installed imagesetters or other output devices.

For this mode of transport to work, the disk drive at the service bureau or printer must be capable of reading your removable hard disk. One manufacturer of removable hard disk systems, SyQuest Technology, has established a de facto standard in the electronic publishing market. SyQuest manufactures drives and removable disks that conform to the standard, and also allows other companies to make compatible drives. Almost all service bureaus have SyQuest drives, and most of their customers do as well.

Magneto-optical disks
are available in 3 1/2
and 5 1/4 inch size.

SyQuest drives come in several varieties, and all are not necessarily compatible with each other. Many users have the older 44-megabyte SyQuest drives, but SyQuest also offers 88-megabyte and 200 megabyte versions of its disks and drives. The older drives can read and write 44-megabyte SyQuest disks but not the 88- and 200-megabyte variety. All of the 200- and 88-megabyte SyQuest drives can read data from 44- or 88-megabyte SyQuest disks. However, the newer drives cannot write data to the older media as fast as can the older drive. Just to make things more confusing, SyQuest also offers drives that use 3.5-inch disks instead of the larger 5.25-inch media. The two formats are incompatible.

SyQuest's archrival in the removable mass storage market is a company called Iomega. Iomega offers a wide range of capacities for its removable Bernoulli disks, all the way up to 230 megabytes. Unlike the SyQuest media, the Iomega drives are compatible with all Iomega disks. However, relatively few service bureaus have the Iomega drives, making them less useful as transport media. Iomega has tried to address this problem by giving its drives away to service bureaus on the theory that the service bureau customers will then buy the drives for themselves. Iomega also offers an inexpensive 3.5-inch removable storage system called the ZipDrive with disks available in 25- and 100-megabyte capacities. But if you are tempted to buy a Bernoulli or ZipDrive, be sure that your service bureau has one.

Magneto-Optical

Magneto-optical drives use a combination of magnetic and optical storage technology. Manufacturers of these drives have targeted the graphic arts market, specifically service bureaus, in competition with SyQuest drives. The advantage of these drives is their high storage capacity, which ranges from 128 to 230 megabytes for the 3 1/2 inch disks and 1.3 gigabytes for the 5 1/4 inch disks. The drives and media tend to be more expensive than SyQuest products

Shuttle drives allow you to remove the hard disk drive from a bay and transport it to another bay.

on an absolute basis, but are less expensive on a cost-per-megabyte basis.

The 128- and 230-megabyte magneto-optical drives are based on international accredited standards. This means that any manufacturer's drive can read from and write to any other manufacturer's disk. (An accredited standard is one established by international standards-setting bodies that employ rigorous methodologies to ensure that no company has an advantage in using the standard. A de facto standard, such as SyQuest, is an informal standard established because a certain company's products dominate a market.)

The major disadvantage of magneto-optical drives is that they are somewhat slower than SyQuest drives, but this is of questionable importance if you are using the disks to transport images to a service bureau.

As with removable hard disks, the major consideration is whether your service bureau or printer can accept the media. Although SyQuest drives are the most common in service bureaus and printers, many imaging services are turning to magneto-optical drives.

Shuttles

Shuttles are another form of removable mass storage technology. In a shuttle, a removable cartridge houses both the disk and drive mechanism. A bay connected to the computer serves merely to move data into the system. Although the shuttle drives are relatively expensive, the empty bays are low-cost, giving users the option of shuttling one large drive around among two, three, or more bays.

Depending on the system used, the hard disk in shuttles can store large amounts of data: 1, 2, 4 gigabytes or more. The drives are also very fast. For this reason, some imaging services use shuttles as a high-speed alternative to local-area networks. They can scan a high-resolution image to a shuttle, carry it to another computer, and bring the image up much faster than they could using a network. However, there are as yet no standards in this market:

shuttles from one manufacturer will not work with bays from another. For this reason, shuttles are of limited use as a transport mechanism. However, if you use very large images and work exclusively with a single service bureau with a specific manufacturer's shuttle, you may find this to be an efficient means of transporting files.

One other storage medium we have not mentioned is tape. Some prepress shops use tape drives to store and transport images. DAT, or digital tape, cassettes are also becoming popular. As with shuttles, tape drives are used mostly for storing and transporting images within a service bureau operation, especially those that use proprietary press systems from Scitex, Screen, or other vendors.

In this chapter, we have neglected one peripheral device that will have a great deal of influence over the ultimate quality of images produced with your scanner: the printer. We believe that image output is important enough that it deserves its own chapter. But before we get to that, we need to discuss how images are captured, edited, and used. Those are the subjects of the next three chapters.

CHAPTER 4

Capturing the Image

You've just installed your new scanner. You're ready to convert your family album of photographs into digital images so you can publish your life story. You slip the first photo into the scanner and look in earnest for the Scan button. Then you discover—there isn't one.

You might think that a tome called *The Color Scanner Book* would be all about hardware. After all, the last chapter dealt with hardware and little else. But getting the most out of your scanner means mastering software. Not just a single software package, but many different kinds of software: scanning software, image-editing software, page layout software, perhaps illustration, presentation, or multimedia software.

Software will provide the focus for the rest of this book, at least until we reach our discussion of output. We begin with this chapter because you will use software, not hardware, to control how the image is scanned.

Just as they have in so many other areas, developers have made tremendous strides in improving the software used to capture images. Some packages allow you to control many variables in the scanning process while offering automated functions that allow you to capture images with nary a thought about brightness, contrast, or other scanning parameters. Many scanning packages sold these days include calibration, color correction, and moiré removal functions that automatically fix the image without requiring any user intervention. Some scanning packages can be run as modules from within popular image-editing programs like Adobe Photoshop.

Almost all scanners are sold with some kind of scanning software. Some manufacturers offer their own scanning software, while others provide packages designed by third-party developers. Many vendors "bundle" their scanners with image-editing programs like Photoshop that include built-in scanning functions. These functions are provided by small programs called "plug-ins" that work with Photoshop and other software.

Another option is the TWAIN interface, which was developed in 1991 by a group of manufacturers to promote broader compatibility between scanners and scanning software. Any scanner that supports TWAIN will work with any software package that also supports the interface. The technology, which stands for "Technology Without An Interesting Name," is especially popular in the Windows environment.

In this chapter, we'll examine the process of capturing an image with your desktop scanner. You'll learn about the different kinds of images that can be captured, the settings to use when scanning these images, and the file formats used to store them. We'll also discuss the process of scanner calibration.

Types of Images

Scanners can be used to capture three kinds of images: line art, continuous-tone, and halftone. We first described these categories in Chapter One. Just to refresh your memory:

"Line art" is a friendlier way of referring to single-bit images. A line art image consists of just two colors, usually black and white, with no intermediate shades of color or gray. The name conjures visions of schematic diagrams and other line drawings, but line art images can contain solid black shapes and patterned backgrounds as well. Line art images are simple enough that almost any kind of scanner can produce high-quality reproductions. Compared with other kinds of images, they make a scanner's job easy.

A continuous-tone image is one in which each area of the image can be a different color or gray shade. The most common example is a photographic print or slide. Some digital output devices, such as dye-sublimation printers, can also produce continuous-tone images.

A halftone is an image consisting of small dots. The dots can be square, round, or oval, but there is always an equal distance from the center of one dot to the center of the next. Dots in light areas of the image are very small, while dots in dark parts of the image are large—something you can verify if you hold a newspaper photo under a magnifying glass. The varying dot sizes create something of an optical illusion. They blend together and fool the unaided eye into perceiving continuous gray shades. The halftone ends up looking much like the original photograph.

Photographs must be converted to halftones because most printing processes cannot vary the intensity of the ink they lay on a page. As a result, they cannot print continuous-tone images. The halftone offers a way to approximate continuous-tone images in print. Using a scanner and imagesetter, you can create a digital halftone. However, halftones can also be created by traditional means using a graphic arts camera. This is how printers did things in the old days before computers came along and made their lives more complicated.

A halftone is sometimes referred to as a screened image, a term that goes back to the old days when the photograph was shot through a screen to convert it into a halftone. The resolution of a halftone is known as its line screen or screen frequency.

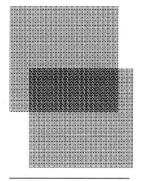

A moiré pattern results when you scan a picture that has already been halftoned because you are superimposing one screen frequency (the scanning resolution) over another screen frequency (the halftone line screen).

Scanners can do a good job of capturing line art and continuous-tone images (provided they have 24-bit color or 8-bit gray-scale capability). However, many scanners have trouble with halftones. The problem is that most scanned images end up being printed as halftones. When you take an image that has already been screened and print it again as a halftone, you essentially superimpose one screen on top of another. The result is an unsightly grid known as a "moiré pattern." Moiré patterns can also arise if you try to scan and print an photograph containing patterned fabrics or another material with a regular, grid-like texture.

Some scanning programs include automatic moiré-removal functions. When you scan the halftone, the software analyzes the screen pattern and reconstructs it into a continuous-tone image. The results are not quite as good as what you would get with a continuous-tone original, but are better than what you'd get with a scanned halftone.

Scanner Control Software

Though they all have their own look, most scanner control packages are remarkably similar in the functions they offer. You begin by launching the program, either as a standalone application or from within an image-editing program. You then have several options for controlling the scan. These options typically include image type, image area, resolution, image scaling, and brightness and contrast. We'll discuss each of these settings in detail.

Image Type

This is usually the first setting you will choose because it will determine what you do with the rest of the settings. We noted above that images can be line art, continuous-tone, or halftone. When choosing image type from your scanner control program, the options are usually a little different. Assuming that you have a color scanner, you can probably choose to scan line art, gray-scale, or color. Obviously, if you have a gray-scale scanner, your options will be limited to line art or gray-scale. Some scanner programs use "black and white" to refer to the line art option.

Choosing image type will help determine the file size of the scanned image. If you choose line art, the size will be relatively small. All other settings being equal, a gray-scale image will consume eight times as much space, and a color image 24 times as much as a line art scan. However, we will see below that you will generally use different

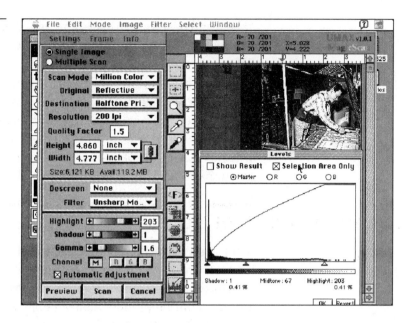

Scanner control software allows you to set scanning and image parameters.

settings for resolution and image size when scanning gray-scale or color images.

Some scanner control programs give you the option of selecting 16 or 256 gray levels in a gray-scale image. If you are scanning a black-and-white photograph, you should opt for the latter. However, the 16-gray-level option can be handy if you are scanning a logo or illustration with a few spot colors that you intend to reproduce in black and white. Assuming there is a high level of contrast between the colors, each will be reproduced as a different gray shade. The advantage of a 16-gray-level image is that it consumes much less disk space than a 256-gray-level image.

In addition to line art, gray-scale, and color, some scanner control programs offer a "halftone" scanning option. The term, in this context, can be somewhat confusing. It may refer to a moiré-removal function that allows you to scan a printed halftone. However, it more likely refers to an option that allows you to produce a "dithered" image. In other words, this option will allow you to convert a continuous-tone image into a halftone as it is scanned instead of when it is printed.

Instead of sensing the image as a series of colors or gray shades, the software converts it into a series of dots, larger dots in dark areas and smaller dots in light areas. There are two problems with this. One is that the image becomes locked into this dot pattern. If you try to enlarge or reduce it later, a moiré pattern will result. The other problem is that the image has a limited resolution. Even if your scanner is capable of 300- or 400-dpi resolution, the screen frequency of the halftone will be much less than this. Some scanning programs will give you options for how the dot pattern is created. Coarse Fatting, for example, simulates a relatively high number of gray shades at a cost in resolution. The Bayer pattern, on the other hand, simulates fewer gray shades but higher resolution.

You should use an option like this only if you have an old scanner that lacks gray-scale or color capability. However, if you have such a scanner, you probably shouldn't be scanning photographic images anyway.

Another useful function of some scanner control programs is the ability to perform batch scanning. After you have done a prescan, the software lets you identify several different rectangular regions in the document and predefine file names for each rectangle. When you click the scan button, several images are scanned to disk without your intervention. In some programs, you can even establish different sets of scanning parameters for each of the rectangular regions you have defined.

Image Area

Once you have selected the image type, you are ready to select the image area: the portion of the image you want to scan. This usually requires a preview scan.

Most scanner programs offer preview scanning as an option. Instead of scanning the image at full resolution, the software scans it at a lower resolution, or in gray-scale instead of color, to speed the scanning process. You can then see a representation of the image in a preview window. If the image is crooked or otherwise needs to be moved, you can correct the problem before you go further.

Watch for Transparent Originals

APPLICATION BRIEF

When you are scanning images from a two-sided document that is printed on relatively thin paper, such as newsprint or tissue, be careful that your scanner does not inadvertently pick up image information from the reverse side of the sheet. A good way to avoid this is to place a blank sheet of paper over the back side of the page being scanned.

After you perform the preview scan, the software allows you to determine which portion of the image you want for the final scan. You usually do this by drawing a frame around the desired segment. Once you are satisfied with the scanning area, you can determine the other scan settings, then click on a button to perform the final scan.

The preview scan in combination with image area selection is a good way to save file space. It doesn't make any sense to scan an entire photograph if you know that it will be cropped later. Many scanner programs show you the file size that will be consumed given the current settings (more on that below). You can see that cropping the image after the preview scan can cut file size considerably.

Resolution and Image Scaling

These settings allow you to determine the resolution of the image—the number of dots per linear inch—and the degree to which the image should be enlarged or reduced.

Scaling factors are usually entered as percentages or absolute sizes. For example, if the original is a 2 x 4-inch print and you want to double its size, you would enter either "200 percent" or "4 x 8" to indicate the final dimensions. If you want to halve it, you would enter "50 percent" or "1 x 2."

Resolution and scaling settings are really two sides of the same coin. An image scanned at 150 dpi at a 100-

percent scale factor is identical to an image scanned at 300 dpi with a 50-percent scale factor.

Choosing the correct settings for these variables can be confusing, especially if you are scanning photos. If you are scanning line art, you generally want to scan at the highest possible resolution. If you plan to scan a gray-scale or color image for final output on a continuous-tone printer, you may want to scan at maximum resolution as well. But if you plan to produce an image as a halftone, scanning at maximum resolution can waste a lot of file space.

When scanning an image that will eventually be printed as a halftone, you need to create a file that includes all of the image data you need and no more. To determine how much data you need, you have to know something about how the image will be printed. The assumption here is that you plan to produce the image on a PostScript imagesetter, but the same technique applies with other output devices that produce halftones.

There is a relatively simple formula that will help you determine the optimal size of the image file you want to create. To keep things simple, we'll use a formula that works with gray-scale images. To figure the settings for color images, multiply everything by three.

$$(\text{Screen frequency})^2 \text{ x image size x 2}$$

In other words, take the screen frequency of the final halftone you want to create, square it (multiply it by itself), multiply this by the number of square inches in the image, and then multiply this by two. The factor of 2 is a "fudge" factor that compensates for the fact that image data is always lost in the sampling process.

Suppose you want to create a halftone with a screen frequency of 100 lines per inch at a size of 2 x 3 inches. The square of 100—in other words, the number of halftone dots in a square inch—is 10,000. An image measuring 2 x 3 inches has a total of six square inches. Multiply six by 10,000 and you get 60,000. Multiply this by two and you get 120,000, or roughly 120 kilobytes. Therefore, you want to create an image file with 120 kilobytes of data.

Most scanning programs make it easy to figure the resolution or scale factor for the target file size by showing you the size of the file that will be created by the scan. As you adjust the resolution or scale factor, the figure changes. However, if your program does not show you the file size, you can figure it out for yourself using this formula:

$$\text{Image size x (scanning resolution)}^2 \text{ x scale factor}$$

Suppose the image we are scanning measures 4 x 6 inches. That's a total of 24 square inches. Suppose we have set the resolution at 150 dpi; 150 squared is 22,500. Multiply the image size by 22,500 and you get 540,000, or 540 kilobytes. Let's suppose we are shooting for a printed image of about 120 kilobytes. So we need to scale down the original image. Using our handy calculator, we find that 120 is about 22 percent of 540. Therefore, we set the scale factor at 22 percent.

Brightness and Contrast

These features are similar to the brightness and contrast controls on a television set. The brightness control allows you to increase or decrease the brightness of an image. You may find, for example, that your scanner tends to darken images. If this is so, you can use the brightness control to compensate for the darkening effect. You can also use the brightness control to lighten a photograph that is too dark to begin with. Keep in mind, however, that there is little you can do if the original image is too light or too dark.

The contrast control allows you to set the degree of difference between light and dark shades in an image. In a high-contrast image, the difference between light and dark is stark. Details may be easier to see, but you may also find that transitions between light and dark portions of the image are not quite as smooth. A low-contrast image may have smoother transitions, but can also have a washed out look.

Determining the optimal level of brightness and contrast is often a matter of experimentation. It also depends on the kind of image you want to scan. For example, when scanning a color photograph on a gray-scale scanner (thus converting it to a black-and-white image), we have found that setting a relatively high contrast works well. You should also set a high contrast when scanning line art.

If your scanner and scanning software allow you to do a prescan, the preview may be enough to indicate the level of brightness and contrast to apply. Usually it is not necessary to keep re-scanning the image. Instead, you can apply various levels of brightness and contrast to the preview image to get at least a rough idea of the effect.

Keep in mind that almost all image-editing programs include brightness and contrast functions that you can apply after the image is scanned. However, it is generally best to get the optimal level of brightness and contrast when the image is scanned.

Some high-end drum scanners include a special function known as "unsharp masking" that improves the clarity of an image as it is scanned. This feature increases the contrast in edge areas of an image, effectively sharpening it. You can get the same effect by applying the "Unsharp Masking" filter in Photoshop or other image-editing programs after the image has been scanned and saved.

Calibration

Many electronic publishing users, especially beginners, are intimidated at the thought of calibrating their scanners. However, calibration is actually a straightforward operation. Some software developers have made the process even easier by including automatic calibration functions in their scanning programs.

In general, calibration is a process in which you measure the accuracy of the scanner, then use your measurements to correct any inaccuracies. By "accuracy," we mean the scanner's ability to accurately reproduce the colors or gray shades in an image. If we determine that the scanner is not accurately reproducing colors, we can correct it. This doesn't mean making any changes to the scanner hardware itself. Instead, we make adjustments to the scanned images to compensate for the inaccuracies.

The Anatomy of an Image

Before we discuss calibration, it would be helpful to examine what might be called the "anatomy" of an image.

A gray-scale image can be divided into three segments: its highlights, shadows, and midtones. The highlights in an image are its lightest portions, the shadows are its darkest portions, and its midtones are the portions in between.

Sometimes we refer to these portions in percentage terms: the highlights might consist of all dots with gray values between 0 and 25 percent, midtones consist of dots with gray values from 25 to 75 percent, and shadows consist of dots with gray values from 75 to 100 percent. You also might hear people refer to "quarter-tones" and "three-quarter-tones," which refer to shades around 25 and 75 percent respectively.

Color images also have highlights, midtones, and shadows, but here things get a little more complicated. A scanned color image is really three images in one: red, green, and blue. Imagine three pieces of transparent film, one with the red portion of the image, the other green, and the third blue. When you place the three pieces of film on top of one another, you get the complete image.

Each of these three layers is sometimes referred to as a "channel." Each channel in an image has its own highlights, midtones, and shadows. When the three channels are combined, the combined image has highlights, midtones, and shadows as well.

If your scanner is perfectly calibrated, the highlights, shadows, and midtones in the scanned image will match the highlights, shadows, and midtones in the original. However, it is rare that a desktop scanner is perfectly calibrated. For example, many scanners have a tendency to darken the midtones in an image. Color images are complicated by the fact that the scanner may darken or lighten the red, green, and blue channels to different degrees.

Calibration Options

The general idea in scanner calibration is to compensate for the scanner's tendency to darken or lighten the shadows, midtones, and highlights in an image. Some scanning programs allow you to make this correction simply by specifying the make and model of the scanner you are using. The software developers have tested popular scanners, figured out the degree to which the scanner inaccurately reproduces colors or gray shades, and then created compensation curves (more on those below) that correct the inaccuracy.

The problem with this approach is that two scanners of the identical make and model might scan midtones, highlights, and shadows differently. For example, one model might be older than another. In addition, you may have a scanner that is not popular enough to have been tested by the software developer. For this reason, many developers have created software that allows you to calibrate individual scanners.

Scanner calibration functions come in many varieties, but the basic approach is the same. First, you scan a special kind of image known as a "target." The target is a slide or page (depending on the kind of scanner you are calibrating) that includes a range of colors or gray shades with known values. In many cases, scanner manufacturers or software developers will provide a special kind of target identified by the cryptic designation "IT8.7." This refers to a standard developed by the American National Standards Institute that establishes just what range of images, colors, and shades should be included in the calibration target.

If the software includes built-in calibration functions, it compares the color or gray-scale values in the scanned

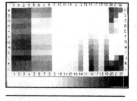

Scanner calibration targets help you calibrate your color scanner by comparing scanned values to standard color samples.

Some scanner control software allows you to set the gamma curve, which automatically adjusts the brightness of different levels within an image.

target with a stored set of reference values. Because the software knows what colors or gray shades the target is supposed to generate, it can measure the difference between these ideal values and the values that were actually scanned. The software then creates something called a "transfer," "compenstation," or "gamma" curve to automatically adjust the scanned image to account for the discrepancy between the scan and the original. For example, if the calibration software reveals that the scanner tends to darken red values, it will automatically lighten those values in the image to compensate.

A gamma curve is sort of like a super brightness control. However, instead of controlling the brightness of the entire image, it can control the brightness of highlights, shadows, and midtones—or even narrower segments— selectively. For example, you can brighten all shades between 30 and 60 percent, but leave the others alone. Or you can darken all shades between 0 and 30 percent while brightening shades between 70 and 90 percent.

"Do-It-Yourself" Calibration

If your software includes automated calibration functions, it will build a gamma curve that automatically corrects for any inaccuracies in the scan. But even if it does not, you can create your own gamma curves to provide a homemade form of calibration. You do this using an image-editing program like Photoshop that includes color mapping functions.

It is also useful to have a device known as a "densitometer," a piece of hardware that measures the amount of reflected light (or transmitted light in the case of a transparency) in an image. You can use a densitometer to measure the gray values in a printed image, then compare the measurements to the values in the scanned image. A similar piece of hardware, a colorimeter, can be used to measure the values in a color image. Some manufacturers have begun to offer inexpensive color-measuring devices that combine the functions of a densitometer and colorimeter. These devices can measure the shades of gray or color in an image and transmit these values directly to the calibration software in a Mac or PC.

Here's how your "homemade" calibration might work: You take a target or other image that includes a wide range of colors or gray shades. Using the densitometer, you measure the colors or gray shades in representative samples of the image. Then you scan the image and import it into an image-editing program like Photoshop.

Photoshop includes an "Eyedropper" tool that allows you to measure the colors in a scanned image by dragging the tool's icon over various portions of it. You then compare the values produced by these measurements with the values generated by the densitometer. If there are discrepencies (as there inevitably will be), you use the software's color mapping function to make the necessary corrections.

The mapping function is usually displayed in the form of a line graph in which the line corresponds to the gamma curve. The x-axis (along the bottom) represents the tonal

Adobe Photoshop's Curves function lets you adjust the gamma or transfer curve, transforming input brightness values to output values.

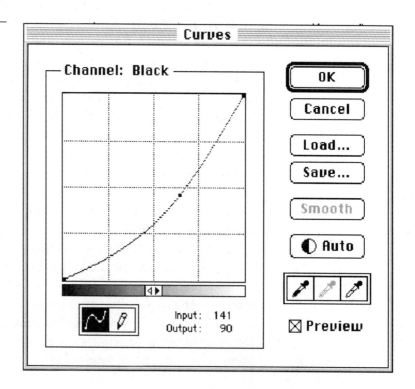

CAPTURING THE IMAGE

values in the original scanned image. The y-axis (along the left) reflects the values in the corrected image—that is, the image that you end up with when you've completed the calibration process. The bottom of the y-axis and left side of the x-axis generally represent black or maximum color density. The top of the y-axis and right side of the x-axis represent white or minimum color density. The gamma curve represents the relationship between the colors or gray values in the original image and those in the corrected image.

If we have not corrected the image at all, the graph displays a straight line from the upper right-hand corner to the lower left. In other words, there is an exact correspondence between the gray shades or colors in both images. A 90-percent shade (near the bottom left of the graph) in the original image is also a 90-percent shade in the corrected image. Now suppose we raise the line a little. That 90-percent shade in the original image is now an 80-percent shade in the new image.

Suppose you scan a target and find that the scanner consistently darkens the midtones by about 20 percent. This happens to be a common problem with many scanners. By raising the line in the midtone area of the graph, we lighten the image in the midtone and thus compensate for the scanner's inaccuracy. Similarly, you can adjust the shadows and highlights if you find that the scanner is also inaccurate in these areas. Depending on how precise you want to be, you can adjust the curve for the entire image, or for the red, green, and blue channels individually. Once you or your software have created a gamma curve, it can be applied to scanned images to automatically make any needed corrections.

Calibration systems offer a precise method for ensuring the most accurate possible color from your scanner. However, many users find that they can often get by with calibrating "by the seat of their pants," so to speak. As they gain experience scanning, modifying, and producing images, they learn about the idiosyncrasies of the various components in their publishing systems and can thus make any necessary adjustments to the image without the need for precise measurements such as those described above. This is especially true in situations where exact color fidelity is not absolutely critical. You might not get the same level of quality that you would from a more scientific approach to calibration, but you may find that the results are "good enough" for your needs.

Color Management Systems

The scanner, of course, is just one component in an electronic publishing system, and many of the other components, especially the display and output device, are just as likely to distort the colors in an image. Recognizing this, several manufacturers have developed what are known as color management systems. These systems are designed to ensure that an image stays as true as possible to the original from the moment it is scanned to when it is printed. It's as if each component adds its own accent to the image; the color management system ensures that the scanner, display, printer, and software are all speaking the same language.

Color management systems typically include device "profiles" that contain information about the color reproduction characteristics of each piece of hardware. This information includes the device's color "gamut"—that is, the range of colors it can produce. Color management systems also use a specific color space as a common reference point. As the image flows through the system, the color management software makes small adjustments to the colors or gray shades to ensure that it is scanned, displayed, and printed with the maximum fidelity.

Some software applications, such as QuarkXPress, come with their own color management software. However, color management is increasingly becoming a function of the system software in a Macintosh or PC. Apple's ColorSync, for example, is built into the system software for the Macintosh. Most scanner vendors provide a device profile for ColorSync, and most Macintosh applications will support the Apple software.

Again, you may find that color management systems represent "overkill" for your particular imaging needs. But they offer one more option for ensuring the highest possible level of quality in your scanned images.

Other Functions

In addition to color-correcting images, some software packages perform other conversions designed to improve the way the image looks when it is finally printed. For example, PixelCraft's ColorAccess automatically converts RGB images into a CYMK format suitable for printing. Some packages also allow you to choose a target output device for the scanned image, making any adjustments necessary to get the best looking image. For example, Adobe Photoshop can convert RGB images into a CYMK format that conforms to the SWOP standard used in the printing industry. This means that the image is converted to a form optimized for reproduction on a printing press (there are actually two SWOP standards, one for printing on coated paper, the other for uncoated paper, but more on that in a later chapter).

Saving the Image

Once an image is scanned, you need to save it in a file on the hard drive. Some scanning programs scan the image into memory, then allow you to save it to disk. Other scanning programs can scan an image directly to a disk file. The latter is generally preferred because you are not limited by the amount of memory in your computer system.

File Formats

Some file formats are unique to the Macintosh, while others are unique to the PC. Some, like TIFF, are used in both environments. The most popular formats are described below.

TIFF

TIFF, short for "Tagged Information File Format," has become the standard for storing gray-scale and color images in both the PC and Macintosh environments. It is widely supported by desktop publishing and computer graphics programs, and is especially preferred if you plan to use a color separation program.

TIFF was developed by Aldus Corp. (now part of Adobe Systems) in cooperation with other developers. Years ago, the format suffered from subtle incompatibilities; not all versions of TIFF were the same, and some programs that could theoretically work with the format had trouble recognizing some of these versions. However, the format has been continually updated and is now remarkably stable.

The TIFF format for the Macintosh is different from the TIFF format for the PC. Some graphics and page layout programs can read either TIFF format, but others can read only the format created for the computer on which it runs. For example, an illustration program that runs on the Macintosh may have problems reading a TIFF file created on the PC. If a software package is available in versions for both the Mac and PC—such as PageMaker or QuarkXPress—it is likely that the program can read either TIFF version. Some software developers offer file conversion packages that can convert a file from PC TIFF to Macintosh TIFF and vice-versa.

PCX

PCX is the file format developed by a company called ZSoft that was a pioneer among developers of PC graphics software. ZSoft no longer exists as a separate company, but PCX remains a popular graphics format in the PC environment. It is supported by many desktop publishing and graphics programs on the PC, though it is still not as widely supported as TIFF. Early versions of PCX were limited to black-and-white images or those with a limited number of colors. However, PCX can now be used to store gray-scale and 24-bit color images.

PICT/PICT2

This is a format developed by Apple Computer for graphics programs that run on the Macintosh. The original PICT format was limited to black-and-white images, but PICT2 supports gray-scale and color. Few PC graphics programs support PICT2, but it is widely supported on the Macintosh. However, many Macintosh users still prefer storing their images in TIFF format.

EPS

EPS, short for Encapsulated PostScript, is a file format capable of handling both bit-mapped and vector-based images. It is based on PostScript, a page description language from Adobe Systems that will be discussed in greater detail in Chapter Seven. PostScript is a programming language that uses English-like commands to describe the creation of pages that can include text and graphics. Most computer graphics programs have the ability to produce PostScript files.

EPS is a special version of PostScript intended to permit exchange of graphic images among different programs and operating systems. Most page layout and illustration programs can import EPS files, but in most cases the files can be printed only on a PostScript output device.

The format is used primarily for object-oriented graphics, but it can also include bit-mapped images from a scanner or other sources. In most cases, EPS is not the preferred format for storing a scanned image because the files generally cannot be edited and tend to be larger than the equivalent TIFF files. But even if you don't save a scanned file directly in the EPS format, it is likely that your images will find their way into an EPS file at some point before they are printed.

There are cases where it makes sense to store your images as EPS files. Some users find that bit-mapped images in EPS files print faster than TIFF files. EPS also allows you to store a bit-mapped image while setting the screen frequency of the eventual halftone. This compares with the TIFF format, where the screen settings are determined by the software that prints the file. This is only a minor advantage for EPS, because in most cases you don't want to set the screen frequency until the image is printed anyway.

There are several variations of the EPS format, some of which offer special advantages when working with bit-mapped images.

The simplest EPS file consists entirely of PostScript commands. However, almost all programs allow you to add a "preview image" to the EPS file. This is a low-resolution bit-mapped image that provides a preview of the file's graphic contents. Without the preview, the file appears as a gray box when you see it on the computer screen. The actual image appears only when the file is printed on a PostScript device. This preview is distinct from any scanned images incorporated into the EPS file. Those images are stored at full resolution.

If an EPS file includes a scanned image, some programs give you the option of saving it with "binary" or "ASCII" encoding. The binary format is generally preferred because it will be substantially smaller than the ASCII format.

Photoshop includes a "bitmap-only" version of EPS, which is unique in that the images can be edited—usually in Photoshop—after they are saved. Yet another variation is the Adobe Illustrator 1.1 format, which can be opened and edited using Adobe Illustrator, Macromedia FreeHand, or other illustration programs. However, this format cannot be used to store bit-mapped images.

The DCS (Desktop Color Separation) format, originally developed by Quark, is a variation on EPS designed for production of color separations from page layout applications. The format is actually five (or more) images in one. The original version of the format, DCS 1.0, consisted of five EPS files—one each for cyan, yellow, magenta, and black plus a fifth file containing a low-resolution screen preview. The idea was that you could work with the low-resolution version in your page layout while retaining links to the larger full-resolution image. DCS 2.0 incorporates all of the process colors—plus optional spot colors—in a single file.

MacPaint

MacPaint was another format created by Apple. It was originally developed for Apple's MacPaint graphics software, but can be created by many Macintosh paint programs in addition to MacPaint itself. The problem with MacPaint is that files are limited to storing black-and-white images at 72-dpi resolution.

RIFF

RIFF is a file format created by a company called Fractal Software (now Fractal Design) for one of the first image-editing programs, ImageStudio. ImageStudio has since been retired, but RIFF is also used in its successor program, ColorStudio. However, ColorStudio also supports TIFF. Because few programs other than ColorStudio or Fractal Painter support RIFF, this file format is not widely supported by scanning programs.

BMP

BMP is the standard bit-mapped format used in Microsoft Windows. One reason to save an image in BMP format is if you wanted to use it as "wallpaper"—that is, a background for the Windows screen. BMP is also supported in the OS/2 operating system.

GIF

This format was created by CompuServe for storing bit-mapped images intended for transmission over phone lines. Only a few scanning programs are capable of creating GIF files. In general, you should use this format only if you want to make files available on a computer bulletin board or online service.

Targa

This format, developed by TrueVision, was one of the first file formats capable of storing 24-bit color. It has since been overtaken by TIFF, but is still supported by many scanning programs.

Image Compression

One of the running themes in this book is the large size of scanned images. Even with the increased capacity of hard drives, a few scanned images can quickly fill your disk. One way to avoid this is to use image compression. Image compression is a process by which image files are reduced to a smaller size. Once reduced, they can be stored more economically, but you cannot use them unless you proceed to decompress them.

Compression techniques fall into two categories: "lossless" and "lossy."

Lossless Compression

In lossless compression, the image is compressed without any loss of image data. When you decompress the image, it will be identical to the form it was in when it was first compressed. The downside is that the degree of compression is generally limited to a maximum of about 50 percent. In other words, the file size can be cut in half, but not much further.

The most popular lossless compression format on the Macintosh is the StuffIt format. This was developed by a fellow named Raymond Lau who created a program called StuffIt for compressing and decompressing files. StuffIt was originally a "shareware" program. "Shareware" is a form of inexpensive software that can be freely copied and distributed from one user to another. If you like the software, you are supposed to send a nominal fee to the developer. Because it worked so well and was so widely available, StuffIt became a de facto standard. An enhanced version of the program called StuffIt Deluxe is available as a commercial off-the-shelf package.

Aldus PageMaker includes its own built-in lossless compression function. When you place an image in a PageMaker page layout, you can choose to convert it to the compressed format.

The PC has two popular lossless compression formats: ZIP and ARC. Again, both formats are supported by shareware programs widely available to PC users through bulletin board services and user groups. ZIP is created by a program called PKZIP. Some file management programs for the PC, such as XTree Gold, include built-in functions for compressing and decompressing files in the ZIP and ARC formats.

One thing to keep in mind is that different compression formats are generally incompatible with each other. For example, if you compress an image in the ZIP format, you need a program that supports that format to decompress it. In most cases, TIFF files that have been compressed with PageMaker's built-in compression function must be decompressed with PageMaker as well.

Lossy Compression

Lossless compression works with nearly any kind of computer file. But as noted above, you are limited in the degree to which you can compress a file. This led some developers to create an alternative form of compression known as "lossy."

Lossy compression schemes were developed specifically for images. The idea was that users needed a way to compress image files at ratios greater than 50 percent. To achieve these higher compression ratios, it is sometimes necessary to throw away some of the data in the image. However, the data is thrown away in a manner where it is difficult or impossible to tell any difference in the image once it is decompressed.

The most popular form of lossy image compression is known as "JPEG," short for Joint Photographic Experts Group. This was a group of companies that got together under the auspices of an international standards-setting body to create an accredited standard for lossy compression.

JPEG offers you the option of compressing an image at various ratios. The more you compress it, the more data you lose. If you compress the image a little, the loss of image data is barely noticeable. But if you compress it by a high ratio, say 50:1, picture quality may be noticeably degraded.

One problem with JPEG is that it comes in different flavors. If you create a compressed JPEG file in one program, you may not be able to decompress it with another program even if the second package supports JPEG. However, certain flavors of JPEG have become standards. Apple's QuickTime system software for the Macintosh includes built-in JPEG compression/decompression for PICT files, and Adobe Photoshop can saves files directly in a JPEG format that is also widely supported. Photoshop can also read a wide range of JPEG flavors beyond the version directly supported by the software.

JPEG compression products come in many forms. Some software packages, such as Photoshop, offer JPEG compression and decompression as part of a larger suite of features. Other programs, such as Storm Technology's PicturePress, perform compression and decompression functions and little else. Some companies offer boards that speed up the compression and decompression process. Some can perform the compression/decompression operation as fast as 30 images per second, matching the speed of standard video.

One compression format that's related to JPEG is MPEG. This is a variation of JPEG designed for video or motion picture images.

These compression products make it much easier to handle large image files. But before you perform the image compression, it is likely that you will want to modify your image in some way. In the next chapter, we will discuss image-editing software.

CHAPTER 5

Modifying the Image

Graphics programs represent one of the largest segments of the microcomputer software market. These packages come in many varieties: illustration programs, paint programs, 3D rendering programs, and so on. But one of the most popular categories of graphics software owes its existence to scanners.

These programs go by several names: photo-editing software, image-editing software, image-processing software, and so on. We prefer the term "image-editing software," but whatever you want to call them, they are designed specifically for modifying color photographs and other images that have been converted into a digital format. But saying that they can "modify" a photograph is sort of like saying that Michelangelo "modified" the ceiling of the Sistine Chapel.

Earlier, we explained how a digital image is nothing more than a collection of numbers. Image-editing programs provide a broad array of tools that allow you to manipulate those numbers in mind-numbing ways. Some, such as Adobe Photoshop, HSC Software's Live Picture, or Micrografx Picture Publisher, represent some of the most sophisticated software developed for microcomputers, allowing you to perform digital magic not unlike the work of the special effects wizards who produced the reality-defying scenes in movies like "Terminator 2" and "Jurassic Park." Others, such as Corel PhotoPaint, are simpler programs that nevertheless offer many functions for modifying scanned images.

Using an image-editing program, you can scan a photographic image, enlarge or reduce it, brighten underexposed areas, darken overexposed areas, remove scratches, and then prepare the image for output on a printer or imagesetter. If an image has a reddish cast, you can reduce the level of red. Or green. Or blue. You can adjust the contrast to bring out otherwise hidden details. You can even create illusions that look like reality: photos of your favorite movie stars with their arms around you, or a shot of your worst enemy dumping toxic waste into the city water supply.

In this chapter, we will outline the features and capabilities found in image-editing programs. Rather than describe each program in detail, we will discuss the features that most of them have in common. As we have noted, these programs are quite complex, and plenty of books are available that provide in-depth guides to popular packages like Photoshop. If you have one of these programs, such books can be valuable complements to the manuals included with the software.

A Brief History of Image-Editing Software

Before we discuss the features in image-editing programs, we thought a little history might be in order. In the first edition of *The Scanner Book*, we described two programs in detail: Letraset's ImageStudio and Silicon Beach Software's Digital Darkroom. A brief discussion of these programs will show how far image-editing software has evolved in just a few years.

Early graphics programs for the Macintosh and PC were known as "paint" packages. They included MacPaint and SuperPaint for the Macintosh, and PC Paintbrush and Dr. Halo for the PC. In their initial releases, these programs were capable of working only with single-bit, black-and-white images. In addition, MacPaint images were limited to 72-dpi resolution.

Paint programs could be used to modify scanned line art and little else. Even with this limitation, they were actually quite useful. You could straighten crooked lines, remove stray dots, and smooth jagged edges in scanned black-and-white images. But modifying photographs—even in gray-scale—was far beyond their capabilities.

Then, in 1987, a company called Letraset introduced a revolutionary program called ImageStudio. Though it bore a superficial resemblance to the earlier paint programs, ImageStudio was designed specifically for working with photographic images.

Instead of painting in black-and-white, ImageStudio allowed you to paint in shades of gray. You could also alter the brightness and contrast of images, convert them into negatives, create composite photographs, even remove people and objects. It included fingerpainting and charcoal tools that mimicked the functions of their real-life counterparts. You could even use sections of an image as painting tools. Image "filters" could be used to perform specialized modifications on the entire image of portions thereof. The Blur filter, for example, caused the image to look as if it were out of focus. A Sharpen filter had the opposite effect, increasing the detail in an image.

ImageStudio was soon joined by a Macintosh-based competitor called Digital Darkroom. This program, developed by a company called Silicon Beach Software, had much in common with ImageStudio. However, it added powerful selection functions like a Magic Wand tool that allowed you to isolate portions of a photograph for cut-and-paste or filter operations. ImageStudio also had selection functions, but they limited the precision with which you could isolate a portion of an image. Another innovation was a "Paste-If" function that allowed you to selectively blend one image into another. A rotation feature allowed you to rotate selected objects in an image. To show the power of this latter tool, the manual used an example in which Italy's famed Leaning Tower of Pisa was straightened—without the need for complex engineering or reconstruction!

At the time they were released, ImageStudio and Digital Darkroom appeared to offer near-miraculous features. It was quite a while before similar programs were developed for the PC. In a testament to the fast-moving nature of the graphics software market, today's image-editing programs make ImageStudio and Digital Darkroom look almost quaint.

Alas, ImageStudio is no more. Several years ago, Letraset decided to largely abandon the Macintosh software market. The company that developed ImageStudio for Letraset, Fractal Software, changed its name to Fractal Design and reacquired the rights to the program. Fractal, which is best known for a "natural media" paint program called Painter, offers a color image-editing program called ColorStudio that is a descendant of ImageStudio. Soon after reacquiring ImageStudio, Fractal retired the package and incorporated its features into a program called Sketcher that combines gray-scale image-editing functions with black-and-white natural media sketching tools like pencils and charcoal.

Digital Darkroom's developer, Silicon Beach Software, was acquired by Aldus Corp. several years ago (which in turn was acquired by Adobe Systems in 1994). An updated version of Digital Darkroom is still available, but it has been overshadowed by other image-editing packages capable of working with color images.

Image-Editing Software Today

Today, the king of the hill in image-editing software is a program from Adobe Systems called Photoshop. First developed for the Macintosh, Photoshop is also available in a version for Microsoft Windows. It is one of the most sophisticated software packages available in any category, with features that allow you to perform a mind-numbing variety of image-editing operations in gray-scale or color. You can also use Photoshop to create images from scratch.

Because Photoshop is so popular, it has spawned a cottage industry of add-on products. Many of these products, known as "plug-ins," add image filters beyond those offered in the basic package. Other plug-ins allow

Crop Your Image As You Scan

APPLICATION BRIEF

It's generally a good idea to crop your images as you scan them, using the preview function of your scanning software, rather than performing this function in software. It makes no sense to carry around excess image data that you have no intention of using.

Don't Crop Too Tight

APPLICATION BRIEF

Despite the previous tip, be careful not to crop your images too tight. Otherwise you may eliminate flexibility you will need later to make the image fit a desired space in your page layout. By carefully cropping your images within your desktop publishing program, you can fill up more space or use less space on your page. But if you haven't scanned a sufficient "safe zone" around your desired target, you may not have the luxury to turn a square image into a horizontal orientation, for example.

you to control a scanner or other image-capture device from within the Photoshop environment. Almost every major scanner manufacturer offers a Photoshop plug-in for its scanners. Many also include free copies of Photoshop as part of the purchase price of their scanners (a practice known as "bundling"). Some offer a simplified version of Photoshop known as the "Limited Edition," while others include the full package.

Photoshop plug-ins have become a de facto standard within the graphics market. As a result, other software developers have designed their packages to accept Photoshop plug-ins. The same plug-ins that work with Photoshop can thus be used with these programs.

Other popular image-editing programs include Corel PhotoPaint and Micrografx Picture Publisher, which are available for the PC under Microsoft Windows. Like Photoshop and ColorStudio, these are sophisticated programs that offer a wide variety of image-editing functions. Micrografx Image Wizard and Caere Corp.'s Image Assistant are simpler and less expensive image-editing programs that still offer many useful features.

One other image-editing program that deserves mention is Live Picture. This program, first developed by a French company called FITS Imaging, uses a revolutionary imaging technology called Functional Interpolating Transformation System (FITS for short). The program is available in the U.S. from a company called HSC Software.

Even on the most powerful microcomputers, image-editing programs can get bogged down when working with large color images—images consuming 100 megabytes or more. For example, rotating a section of an image even a few degrees can take an hour or more, depending on how much memory you have. In Live Picture, these modifications can be made almost instantly. The modifications are stored as mathematical formulas in an underlying file format known as IVUE. In addition to

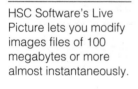

HSC Software's Live Picture lets you modify images files of 100 megabytes or more almost instantaneously.

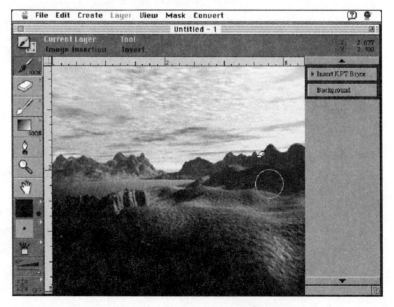

MODIFYING THE IMAGE

Micrografx Picture Publisher is one of the most popular Windows-based image-editing programs.

Corel Photo-Paint is available as a standalone program or bundled with CorelDraw for Windows.

allowing for fast image manipulation, the IVUE format allows you to undo any change made to an image from the moment you began working on it. Once you have completed your work, you can convert the image into TIFF format. The conversion takes some time, but this is much better than waiting for the screen to redraw whenever you have made a minor change to an image.

With its ability to work with such large images in real time, Live Picture gives desktop computers users much of the imaging power found in dedicated graphics workstations like the Quantel Paintbox, which cost hundreds of thousands of dollars. Another recent image-editing program designed for use with large images is xRes from Fauve Software.

Anatomy of an Image Editing Program

Each image editing program uses its own approach to the process of modifying color images. But almost all of these packages have many features in common. They include:

- Painting tools that allow you to draw or paint directly on an image;

- Selection tools that allow you to isolate a portion of an image for cut-and-paste or masking operations;

- Image filters that modify the values of the pixels in an image, providing a wide range of special effects;

- Transformation functions that allow you to rotate, resize, or distort portions of an image; and

- Color correction functions that allow you to modify the colors or gray values in an image.

In addition to these built-in functions, many image-editing packages can be expanded and customized by installing the plug-ins described above.

Painting Tools

Painting tools are designed to simulate the actions of such traditional artist's tools as paintbrushes, airbrushes,

Four-color process printing, such as used in this color section, combines cyan, magenta, yellow, and black plates (below) to create photographic images.

CYAN

MAGENTA

YELLOW

BLACK

A "gamma," or transfer function curve controls the relationship between intensity values captures by the scanner and those sent to the output device. This curve, a straight line, makes no adjustment of the scanned image data.

This curve darkens scanned values in the midtones of the photo.

This curve lightens the midtones.

Color halftones can be produced with different screen frequencies. In general, the higher the screen frequency, the better the quality.

150 lpi

100 lpi

85 lpi

Halftones can be produced with different shapes of dots.

Diamond

Elliptical

Line

The histogram function shows the distribution of tonal values within an image. A four-color image has four separate histograms for each component color plus a fifth composite histogram.

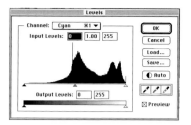
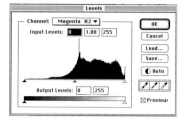
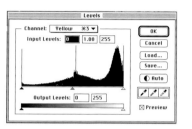
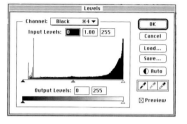

By modifying the black and white points in the original histogram (right), you can compress the range of tonal values contained in an image (below).

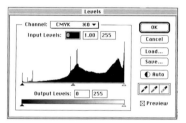
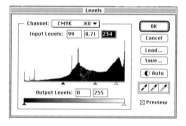

Image-editing programs like Adobe Photoshop offer numerous filters that transform an image.

Unsharp Mask

Blur

Ripple

COLOR INSERT

**Add
Noise**

Extrude

**Find
Edges**

THE COLOR SCANNER BOOK

It is important that photos be scanned with enough image data to support the physical size and line screen you have specified. This image does not have enough image data and thus appears pixelated.

This shows the result of using Photoshop's interpolation function to increase the amount of image data in the photo above.

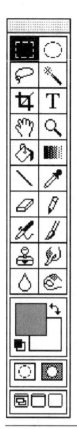

The toolbox in Adobe Photoshop contains several painting, selection, and transformation tools.

and charcoal. Other tools allow you to draw lines, circles, or geometric shapes. They are similar to the tools in the early painting programs, but go much further. For example, in addition to selecting colors from a "palette," you can often select a texture from an image and use that as your "paint."

Painting tools can be used to perform minor touch-ups on an image—such as fixing scratches. You can also use them to create original artwork from scratch. Most image-editing programs allow you to change the width or shape of your painting tools, offering tremendous flexibility in how they work. With some programs, you can even modify such attributes as the transparency of the painting effect or the degree of softness around the edges.

Commonly available painting tools are described below:

Paintbrush. This is a basic tool for adding colors or gray shades to the electronic canvas.

Eyedropper. This is not a painting tool per se, but is used in conjunction with other painting tools. After selecting the tool, you point at an area of the image and the eyedropper automatically "picks up" the color or texture for use with the paintbrush or other tool.

Airbrush. This tool, like a traditional airbrush, "sprays" a mist of tiny dots into the image.

Paint Roller. This tool allows you to quickly fill an area with a selected color or pattern.

Line and Shape Tools. These tools are used to draw perfect lines, curves, or shapes. To create a shape, you typically move the tool to one corner of the shape you want to draw, hold down the mouse button, then drag to the other corner. You can usually choose whether to create a hollow shape or one filled with a selected color or pattern.

Clone. This tool, sometimes known as a Texture tool, is one of the most powerful found in the toolboxes of most image-editing programs. It allows you to recreate one portion of an image in another. First you select an object or area in the image you want to recreate. Then you move the tool to another part of the image and begin drawing. As you move the mouse, the area you first selected is painted into the new area.

Clone tools are especially useful when retouching photographs. Suppose you need to fix a scratch that appears on the side of a brick building in a scanned image. Using the clone tool, you can draw over the scratch using the same brick pattern that appears on the side of the building.

Eraser. This tool allows you to erase portions of an image. However, with some programs it is better to use the paintbrush tool to perform the same function because you generally have more flexibility in determining the width and shape of the paintbrush.

Text Tool. This tool allows you to add text to your artwork. In some programs, clicking on the tool brings up a dialog box into which you can type your text. Other programs allow you to type text directly on the screen. The text tool can be used to create interesting effects, but don't confuse it with the text-entry capabilities in a word-processing program or even an illustration package. Once you have finished entering your text, it becomes part of the image and cannot be changed without erasing it and starting again.

Dodge and Burn. This tool, sometimes known as a Brighten tool, allows you to selectively brighten or darken part of an image. It is useful in situations where a small portion of an otherwise good-looking image may be over- or underexposed. Most image-editing programs also include a brightness function that works on the entire image or a selected area.

Blend. This tool allows you to add smoothing or softening effects. It often appears as a waterdrop, and the effect is similar to adding water to a watercolor painting. It is often used to soften boundaries between high-contrast areas in the image.

Smear. This tool creates a smearing effect. It can be likened to an electronic fingerpaint tool. When you paint over the image, it becomes smeared as if you were running your finger through the fingerpaint.

Selection Tools

Selection tools allow you to select a portion of an image for further image processing applications. You do this by drawing a line (sometimes known as a "marquee") around the part of the image you want to select. A dotted line indicates the portion that has been selected. Once a part of the image is selected, you can perform one of several operations:

Cut or copy the image to the Clipboard. The Clipboard, a feature in the Macintosh and Windows, is a temporary holding area for text or graphics. When you select an area of the image, you can copy it to the Clipboard, then use a Paste command to paste it elsewhere, either in the same file or a different file. When you Cut the selected area, it disappears from the current workspace. When you Copy the area, it remains in the workspace and a copy is placed on the clipboard. Copy-and-Paste features are often used to create composite images—images that combine different elements together. For example, you can copy a photo of yourself into a photo of your favorite movie star.

Transform the selected area. Once a portion of an image is selected, you can drag it around the screen, rotate it, reduce or enlarge it, or distort it.

Mask the selected area. This means that you can restrict subsequent image-editing operations to the area either inside or outside the selected portion of the image. For example, you can select an area of an image that is too dark and use the brightness function or dodge-and-burn tool to brighten it. Or you can restrict the actions of the paintbrush to areas outside the masked portions. Some image-editing programs include highly sophisticated masking functions that can restrict operations to certain colors. Or you can add a fine "screen" to a mask restricting the amount of electronic "paint" that seeps through.

Most image-editing programs include several selection tools:

Shape tools. Like the shape painting tools, shape selection tools allow you to draw regular shapes around the portion of an image you want to select. Common shape selection tools include a box, circle, and polygon. The latter tool allows you to draw a shape consisting of many straight lines.

Lasso Tool. This tool can be used to draw a freehand selection area.

Magic Wand. This tool allows you to automatically select an irregular object by simply clicking inside it. It works best when the colors or gray shades within the object have similar values and there is a high degree of contrast with the surrounding area. Most image-editing programs with Magic Wands allow you to determine the degree of tolerance, that is, the range of color or gray values from the center of the selection area that will be selected. For example, you can click inside a leaf and specify that the tool select all of the color shades within the leaf.

In addition to these tools, many image-editing programs allow you to combine different selections, or remove a portion of a selection.

Image Filters

An image filter is a small program that modifies the pixels in an image to produce some sort of effect. We explained earlier that a digital image is nothing more than a collection of numbers. A filter changes the values of those numbers in a way that produces the desired modification. For example, the Sharpen filter sharpens detail by changing the values of pixels on the borders of objects.

Filters come is staggering varieties, from simple blur or sharpen effects to filters that radically transform the look of an image. In many cases, you can choose the degree to which the effect is applied. Some of the common ones are described here:

Add Noise. This filter creates a grainy, static-like effect by adding random dots to the image. It is sort of like watching the image on a television set with poor reception.

Soften. This filter, sometimes known as a "blend" filter, is used to soften and smooth the colors in an image. If an image appears to have too much contrast between neighboring dark and light areas, this filter will blend the areas together, making the transition smoother.

Sharpen. The Sharpen filter emphasizes the boundaries between neighboring colors in an image, bringing out greater detail.

Unsharp Masking. This filter increases the contrast in edge areas of an image,, producing a lighter and darker line on each side of the edge. It is useful for clarifying out-of-focus images.

Trace Edges. This filter enhances the edges of objects in an image, sometimes converting it into something that looks like a line drawing.

Blur. This filter modifies the image to look as if it were shot through an out-of-focus lens.

Motion Blur. This effect makes the image look as if it were photographed at a high rate of speed. It creates an especially interesting look if you select one object in the image, such as a person, for application of the effect.

Diffuse. This filter produces small random shifts in the pixels in an image. Imagine a sandbox in which images are formed from particles of colored sand. Applying the diffusion filter is like shaking the sandbox to scatter the particles.

Maximum/Minimum. The Maximum filter has the effect of brightening the image by emphasizing lighter areas and causing them to blur into darker areas. The Minimum filter has the opposite effect, darkening the image by emphasizing the darker areas at the expense of lighter shades.

Posterize. This filter reduces the number of gray shades or colors in an image, causing it to appear more like a painting than a photograph. For example, you can choose to posterize a 256-gray-level image to have just 8 gray levels. When you apply the filter, it forces the pixels into one of the selected number of levels.

Remove Spots. This filter searches the image for spots or blotches and removes them. You can usually choose the size of the spots it should look for. If you choose to remove large spots, you may lose portions of an image you want to keep.

Emboss. This filter converts the image into what appears to be a raised relief (like the impression on a rubber stamp). To enhance the 3D illusion, the effect adds shadows and highlights to the image, as if a light source were shining on it.

Mosaic. This filter, sometimes known as a "Pixelation" filter, converts the image into a series of relatively large box-like pixels, as if its resolution were drastically reduced. It's similar to the effect you see on television news shows where they interview someone who doesn't want their face shown.

Most image-editing programs come with a set of standard filters, but if your software supports Photoshop plug-ins, you can vastly expand your selection of filters. Plug-ins, as we mentioned earlier, are small programs that add new capabilities to Photoshop or other software that supports the technology. Numerous companies offer packages of plug-in filters that go far beyond the standard filters described above. One of the most popular of these is Kai's Power Tools from HSC Software, which is available for Macintosh and Windows computers.

Another software package from HSC, KPT Convolver, is a plug-in application that allows you to create your own filter effects. You can experiment with different combinations of standard filters using your own images or those supplied with the program. When you have created an effect you like, you can save it for application to other images.

Transformation Functions

Transformation functions allow you to flip, rotate, or resize the image or selected portions of the image. In most cases, you begin by selecting a part of the image using selection tools, then choose the transformation command.

Flip. This transformation creates a mirror image or inverted version of an image. Flip Horizontal flips the picture along an imaginary vertical axis; the effect is a mirror image. Flip Vertical turns the image upside-down. The Flip Horizontal function can be a lot of fun in combination with the Copy and Paste commands. You can select the outline of a person in a photograph, copy it to the Clipboard, Paste it back in, and Flip it horizontally to create a twin.

Rotate. This command allows you to rotate the entire image or a selected portion. Some programs allow free rotation, meaning you can rotate the selected portion to any degree you want. Others limit the rotation to 90, 180, or 270 degrees. This command often takes a long time to execute.

Resize. The resize options allow you to enlarge or reduce an image or the selected portion of an image. If the program allows free resizing, you can enlarge or reduce the image visually by dragging on handles that appear around the selected area. Or you can enter percentage values to determine the amount of resizing. In most cases, you can choose to keep the image's aspect ratio: that is, the ratio between its height and width. If you don't want to maintain the aspect ratio, you can enlarge or reduce the height or width independently. This has the effect of stretching or compressing the image.

Color Correction Functions

Color correction functions are among the most important in any image-editing program. Many of the functions described above are used to create special artistic or visual effects, or just to have some fun with your scanned images. Color-correction functions are used with everyday images to improve the way they will look when they are eventually printed.

Almost all image-editing programs include simple brightness and contrast controls that work on the entire image or selected portions. Another common feature allows you to convert a positive image into a negative. But most image-editing programs go far beyond this to offer extensive features for modifying the color range and color balance in an image.

These features, which include histogram equalization and color map adjustment, do two things: they provide information about the color or gray values in an image, and offer a way to modify those color or gray values to get the best-looking image possible considering your output device.

Color/Gray Map

In the last chapter, we described the process of scanner calibration. The core of the calibration function is a graph displaying a "transfer," "compensation," or "gamma" curve that modifies the color or gray values in an image. Another term for this graph—especially when it is used for functions other than calibration—is a "color/gray map."

As we noted in the last chapter, you can use this function to fix an image that is too light or too dark in the shadows, midtones, or highlights. But you can also use a color/gray map to create a variety of special effects. For example, if you want to emphasize the red in an image, you can choose the red channel and increase the amount of red by lowering the line (lowering the line has the effect of darkening or emphasizing the values, while raising it lightens or de-emphasizes the values).

You can also use the color/gray map to create an effect known as "solarization" by reversing the gray or color values in the middle of the compensation map while leaving the rest alone. You can also create your own posterization effect similar to that produced by the posterization filter.

Even if the image has been calibrated to account for the tendencies of your scanner, you may want to use the color/gray map to calibrate the image for your output device, printing press, or paper stock. For example, when printing on highly absorbent uncoated papers like newsprint, dots tend to spread more than they do on coated stocks or less absorbent uncoated stocks. This phenomenon is known as "dot gain." The result is that the image appears darker than it should. You can correct this by lightening the image with the color/gray map. Most image-editing programs allow you to save and reload multiple maps, meaning that you can have different maps for different kinds of presses or paper stocks and then load them as needed.

Histogram/Equalization

There are many ways that we can determine how well an image will look in print. One way is simply to look at it on a monitor. Though this is not an entirely accurate predictor of how the image will look, you can tell if there are any obvious problems such as severely under- or over-exposed areas.

However, many image-editing programs offer a more powerful way to obtain information about an image: the histogram. A histogram is a graph that shows the distribution of gray shades or colors in an image. It consists of thin vertical lines arranged along a horizontal axis. Each point on the axis corresponds to a color or gray value moving from white or low density on the left to black or high density on the right. The length of the vertical line tells you how many pixels in the image match that particular gray or color value. A long line means there are a lot of pixels with that value, while a short line means there are few pixels of that value.

A histogram shows the distribution of gray values within an image.

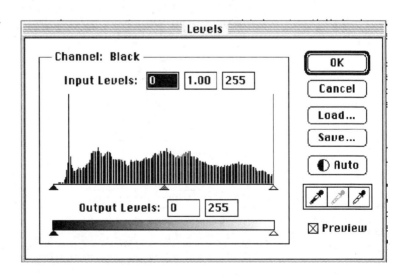

The histogram thus gives you a quick way of telling how gray or color values are distributed in an image. An overexposed image will show many long lines clustered toward the right side of the histogram. A high contrast image will show two separate clusters of long lines, one at each end of the graph.

Ideally, the lines in a histogram should be distributed along the entire graph in a gradual bell-shaped curve. If too many lines are clustered in a small portion of the graph, it is likely that the picture will be lacking in detail. Of course, this is not necessarily true with all images. A shot of a starry sky, for example, will show a lot of long lines clustered toward the dark side of the spectrum with a smaller number of shorter lines closer to the light side. But if the shot is supposed to show a wide range of colors or gray shades, and the histogram indicates there are not, you may have a problem with the photo.

In addition to displaying the histogram, many image-editing programs allow you to modify the values in the histogram through a process called equalization. Equalization redistributes the color or gray values in an image to produce a better range between the lightest and darkest shades.

Prepress Functions

Finally, some of the more powerful image-editing programs offer a way to replicate certain color-correction

Photoshop's Printing Inks Setup dialog box, accessed under Preferences, allows you to compensate for dot gain, the tendency for dots of ink to spread when they hit the page. You can also set up the file to conform to SWOP (Coated), an industry standard for printing on coated stock.

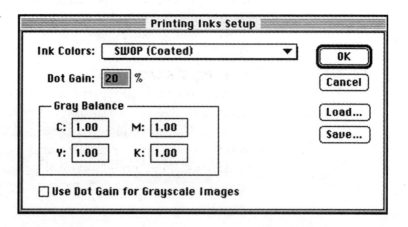

MODIFYING THE IMAGE

In Photoshop, GCR and UCR functions are accessed through the Separation Setup dialog box under Preferences.

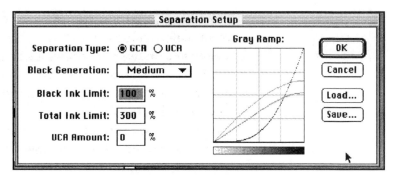

operations traditionally used in the prepress industry. These operations are designed to adjust the balance of inks on press to ensure consistent image quality. The general idea to remove equal portions of cyan, magenta, and yellow and replace them with black. This can be done in one of two ways: undercolor removal (UCR) and gray component replacement (GCR).

In undercolor removal, the black ink is added rather selectively, while gray component replacement adds a greater degree of black. GCR is generally preferred for images with dark, saturated colors. Another operation, undercolor addition (UCA), reduces the degree of undercolor removal in the darkest portions of an image.

The degree of GCR or UCR you should employ is determined in part by the paper and press with which the job is printed. As a result, you should always consult with your printer to learn about any suggestions or requirements they may have in this area. It may not even be necessary to worry about these operations because you can probably get by with the default CYMK conversion function in your image-editing software.

Faster, Faster

Image-editing programs are powerful pieces of software, but they also require powerful hardware to keep from getting bogged down. Scanned images, as we have noted more than once, consume lots of memory, and modifying these images with a program like Photoshop can be a glacial process if your system isn't fast enough to keep up.

Perhaps the best way to boost your system's image-editing performance is to add more random-access memory. In Chapter Two, we recommended that you install three to five times as much RAM as the size of the largest image you intend to work with. If your images come in under two megabytes, you'll do fine with 6 to 10 megabytes of RAM. But if you're working with 20-megabyte images, you'll need anywhere from 64 to 128 megabytes of RAM to work in an efficient manner.

Image filters, and transformations like rotation and re-sizing, are among the most hardware-intensive operations you're likely to perform with an image-editing program. Recognizing this, several manufacturers offer accelerator boards specifically designed for use with Photoshop. These boards include specialized chips that accelerate filter and transformation operations.

Finally, we have noted that HSC's Live Picture and Fauve Software's xRes are both designed for use with scanned images consuming 100 megabytes or more. However, keep in mind that both programs have hefty memory requirements of their own.

In this chapter, we have just barely touched on the capabilities found in image-editing programs. Mastering these programs can be a time-consuming process given their complexity, but also a very rewarding one considering their power. One characteristic of programs like Photoshop is that there are usually several ways to accomplish the same task. For example, you can brighten an image using the color/gray map, brightness control, or dodge and burn tool.

For all their power, image-editing programs are just one stop on the path from scanning an image to producing final output. Unless you are a photographer or fine artist who wants to print the image and nothing else, you probably are planning to use your scanned images in a page layout, slide presentation, multimedia production, or another form of communication. In the next chapter, we will discuss the various programs with which you can use scanned images.

CHAPTER 6

Using the Image

We're near our destination. Our image has been scanned, touched up with an image-editing program, and saved in a standard file format like TIFF. Now we're ready to use it. This means importing the image into one of several kinds of programs. It might be a page layout program, a presentation program, an illustration program, or even a multimedia or digital video system. This will be the last stop on the image's journey to a printer, imagesetter, film recorder, or other output device.

In this chapter, we'll look at how you can use scanned images once they've been modified to your satisfaction. We'll discuss several software categories in which scanned images may be used, with a focus on page layout packages. We'll pay special attention to features in these programs designed for use with scanned images. Then, in the next chapter, we'll discuss printing and reproduction of scanned images.

First, there is a rather sticky issue we need to discuss: one regarding copyright laws.

Legal Issues

Before you go inserting reproductions from the Metropolitan Museum of Art into your corporate newsletter, you should take a few moments to consider the legal ramifications of scanned images. Most pictures that appear in commercial publications, including photographs, line art, and other illustrations, are copyrighted by the publisher. Legally, scanning such an image for use in a publication violates the copyright. If your publication is not for profit and is distributed to a limited audience, you probably don't have much to worry about. But if you are scanning images for a commercial purpose, be careful to honor all copyrights. Read the copyright notice carefully; it may define allowable uses of the intellectual property covered.

Some images are in the public domain and thus are not copyrighted. For example, images printed in publications that are more than 60 years old are generally safe to use because the copyrights have expired. These images can be scanned and used as desired. But you should still be absolutely sure that the copyrights no longer apply.

There are also legal questions raised by the ability to alter an image once it is scanned in. How many changes must be made to an image before it is considered a new work of art? If you scan in an illustration and modify it to the point of being unrecognizable, it is doubtful that you will be sued for copyright violation. But anything is possible.

It pays to be careful. Many publishers will happily give you permission to reprint images, as long as you give them proper credit. Be sure to get permission, in writing if possible, if you have any doubts about using an image found in someone else's publication.

Now that we've got the legalese out of the way, let's discuss your many options for using scanned images.

Page Layout Programs

Page layout programs, also known as desktop publishing programs, are software packages geared toward the production of such print materials as newspapers, magazines, newsletters, brochures, flyers, books, and catalogs. Early page layout programs were generally limited to black-and-white or spot color output and had limited graphics-handling capabilities. However, the current generation of page layout software offers powerful functions for importing, handling, and producing color images.

Page layout programs vary widely in price and capability. Some are geared primarily toward long, structured, technical documents. Others are geared toward shorter publications like brochures and newsletters. The most popular programs, Aldus PageMaker and QuarkXPress, offer features that combine these capabilities to varying degrees. Low-cost page layout programs like Microsoft Publisher offer relatively limited feature sets, but also require less learning time. They are suited mostly for producing flyers and other simple one-page documents.

Some graphical word processing programs, notably Ami Professional and Microsoft Word for Windows or the Macintosh, offer many of the same publication-oriented features found in low-end page layout programs. These packages are suitable for newsletters and other simple publications, and most have the capability to import scanned images, at least in black-and-white. However, for lengthy documents or four-color work you'll need a more powerful program dedicated to page layout.

It's useful to think of page layout programs as meeting places for all of the elements that comprise a publication. Most have extensive import filters that allow them to work with text and graphics created in a wide range of applications: word processors, illustration programs, image-editing packages, sometimes even database or spreadsheet programs (especially for catalogs, directories, or financial documents). These include filters capable of importing scanned images in TIFF, PICT, or other file formats.

Once an image is placed in a page layout, almost all of these programs offer tools that allow you to re-size or crop it. Some programs also offer simple image control functions that work in a similar manner to the color/gray map editors in Photoshop.

Some page layout programs also support a handy feature called automatic picture replacment (APR). APR works like this: your service bureau scans an image at high resolution, then creates a copy at low resolution. You get the low-resolution version, while the service bureau keeps the original high-resolution version. You can then import the image into your page layout program and position it on the page. You can also scale or crop the image, though you cannot modify it with an image-editing program. Because it is a low-resolution "position only" image, it consumes relatively little file space and doesn't slow down your system the way a high-resolution image would. When you submit the page layout file to the service bureau for color separation, the service bureau's software automatically replaces the low-resolution image with the high-resolution original—scaled and cropped just as it was in your page layout.

To perform this magic, your service bureau probably uses what is known as an "OPI print server." OPI, which stands for "Open Prepress Interface," was developed by Aldus Corp., originally for use with high-end prepress systems. The picture swapping capability described here is one of the nicest features of OPI. The OPI software resides on the server, which is essentially a computer system designed to manage file output in a service bureau.

Even without OPI, most page layout programs offer a feature that allows you to avoid performance bottlenecks when a large scanned image has been placed on the page. Instead of displaying the image at full resolution—which tends to slow screen redraws—you can choose to have the image shown at low resolution or not at all. In the latter case, a gray box appears in place of the picture. The image hasn't gone anywhere—it will still print at full resolution—but your computer doesn't have to do quite as much work to show the image on the screen.

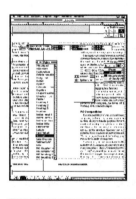

PageMaker was one of the first desktop publishing programs.

The most popular page layout packages on the market are QuarkXPress, Adobe PageMaker, Corel Ventura, and FrameMaker. Each of these programs is profiled below, with a focus on their ability to work with scanned images.

Adobe PageMaker

Adobe PageMaker is by most measures the most popular desktop publishing program on the market. Developed by Aldus Corp. before that company was acquired by Adobe, it was one of the first software packages in this category and helped launched what has come to be known as the "desktop publishing revolution." It was also the first desktop publishing program to be available in both Macintosh and PC-compatible versions. The PC version of PageMaker runs under Microsoft Windows.

One of PageMaker's major strengths is its highly intuitive user interface. When you launch the program, you are presented with an electronic version of a pasteup board. You can move items on or off the board as if you were working on a real-life art table. A movable toolbox on the screen provides access to tools for adding text and graphic elements. The toolbox also features a cropping tool.

Graphic images (and text) are imported into PageMaker using a "Place" command. You select the command from the File menu, after which you are asked to specify the name of the file to be imported. Files can be imported either as independent or inline graphics. An independent graphic can be moved anywhere on the screen, while an inline graphic becomes part of the text. When the text moves, the graphic moves with it.

PageMaker's Image Control dialog box let's you perform basic image editing functions.

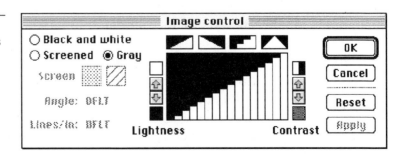

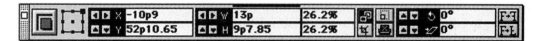

PageMaker's Control Palette lets you enter precise values for image sizing, scaling, and placement.

Images that are relatively small are incorporated directly into the PageMaker file. Large color images, however, are "linked." Instead of storing the image in the file, PageMaker links it to the publication. If you copy the file to a diskette or removable hard disk for transport to a service bureau, you must also copy the graphic image or it won't be available when the service bureau opens the file.

PageMaker offers several options for manipulating graphics once they are imported. You can crop the image using the cropping tool. Simply select the tool, click in the middle of the image, and drag on the handles that appear around the image to crop on any of the four sides. One nice thing about the cropping feature is that you can easily "uncrop" the image by dragging the handles back to the original position. It's sort of like a window shade that can be opened or closed to reveal or hide the scene outside.

Images can be easily resized in PageMaker by clicking on them with the arrow tool. A set of handles appear just as they do with the cropping tool. However, instead of cropping the image, moving the handles causes the image to grow larger or smaller. You can maintain the aspect ratio—the ratio between the height and width of the image—by holding down the Shift key as you drag on the handles.

The Control Palette in PageMaker also makes it easy to scale or crop an image simply by typing in a percentage enlargement value for both the horizontal and vertical dimensions.

PageMaker includes an Image Control function that allows you to perform simple modifications on certain kinds of images. If you have properly prepared your file in an image-editing program, you won't need to use this function, but it's nice to know it is there.

PageMaker, like other programs, has gone through a lengthy series of upgrades since it was first released. In early versions of PageMaker, the Image Control function

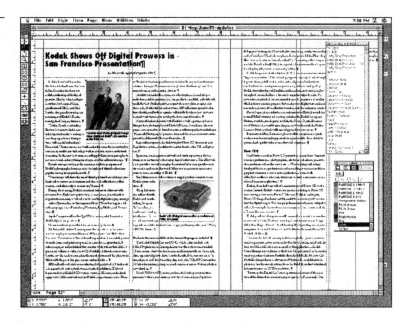

QuarkXPress uses frames to hold pictures such as scanned images.

worked only with gray-scale images. In addition, early versions of PageMaker for the PC could not produce color separations. If you are using one of these versions, you will probably be limited to working with gray-scale images. However, recent versions of PageMaker have sophisticated color imaging capabilities.

QuarkXPress

QuarkXPress has long been PageMaker's chief rival in the Macintosh environment. With its powerful functions for handling type and graphics, it has been a favorite among professional graphic designers. Quark also offers a version of QuarkXPress for Microsoft Windows.

QuarkXPress handles graphics a little differently from PageMaker. Instead of using a Place command to import the image and position it on the page, XPress uses what are known as "picture boxes." You click on the picture box icon on the screen, then draw the box on the page. Once you draw the box, you can then import the graphic. You can choose from several Picture Box shapes, including round, square, or polygonal, or create your own.

Cropping and scaling are also handled a little differently. When you create the picture box and import the graphic, you can place the graphic entirely within the boundaries of the box, or have it sit behind the box as if it is being viewed through a window. If you choose the latter option, you can move the image so that different portions "peek" through the window. You can resize the image by calling up a Picture Box dialog box and entering reduction or enlargement values.

QuarkXPress offers powerful color output functions. Quark also offers an Image Control function, similar to the one in PageMaker, that works with color or gray-scale images. Again, it should not be necessary to use this function if you have done a good job of correcting your image in your image-editing program.

QuarkXPress also includes a built-in color management system called EFIcolor from a company called Electronics for Imaging. EFIcolor automatically adjusts images in QuarkXPress so they will look as good as possible on output.

Corel Ventura

Ventura Publisher was one of the first popular page layout packages for PC-compatible computers. Though it is not the easiest program to learn, it can be quite productive once you master its approach to document design. It is especially strong for producing books, reports, and other long documents with a consistent format. However, it can also be used for producing newsletters, flyers, and other publications with smaller page counts.

The program was originally developed by a small California company called Ventura Software, which sold the marketing rights to Xerox Corp. Xerox then sold the package as "Xerox Ventura Publisher." In 1990, Xerox took over development of the program and established a subsidiary in San Diego known as Ventura Software to sell and support the package. Then, in 1993, Xerox sold the rights to the program to Corel Corp., the company responsible for CorelDraw. The current version of the program runs under Microsoft Windows.

Ventura uses a frame-based approach to page layout. A frame is a block on the page layout that can contain text or graphics. To import a graphic, you select the Frame tool, draw the frame on the page, then select the file to be imported. You can then crop or scale the image using commands in the Frame menu.

When Ventura places an image into a frame, it must make some decisions. It can place the image at its original size, without regard to the size of the frame, or it can try to fit the image into the frame dimensions. If it places the image at the original size, the frame (assuming it is smaller than the image) acts like a window, allowing you to see only a portion of the image at any one time.

If the image is forced to fit into the frame, Ventura makes another decision. It can maintain the aspect ratio, that is, the ratio between the image's height and width, or it can allow the aspect ratio to be distorted. Suppose you have a horizontal image that measures 4 x 6 inches. If you try to fit that image into a 6 x 4 frame—a vertically oriented area—Ventura distorts it. Objects within the image will appear thin and stretched out. If the aspect ratio is maintained, Ventura reduces the photo so that it fits within the frame without distortion. Because the proportions of the frame and image are different, some white space will be left at the bottom or top of the frame.

Ventura can resize an image in one of two ways. You can manually resize a frame by clicking on its handles and dragging with the mouse, or you can enter numeric values in a dialog box that tell the program how much to reduce or enlarge the image.

FrameMaker

Frame Technology's FrameMaker is derived from a technical publishing package first offered for Unix-based workstations. It was originally developed for production of technical manuals and other long, structured documents, and these remain its forte.

FrameMaker imports graphic images primarily in the TIFF format. Early versions of FrameMaker had weak color imaging features, but with version 4, Frame enhanced the program's color imaging functions considerably.

Graphical Word Processors

Graphical word processors like Ami Professional and Microsoft Word for Windows combine word processing functions with page layout features that rival those in some desktop publishing programs. Both of these programs run under Microsoft Windows and are quite popular.

These programs include two modes for creating documents. In draft mode, you simply enter text as you would in a conventional word processing program. But you can also work in a layout mode that allows you to add images and other graphic elements. Working in layout mode, you can create many of the same kinds of documents you can create with a page layout program.

These programs are generally weak in their color functions, especially when it comes to four-color output. While a user of a page layout program is likely to employ a service bureau to produce high-resolution imagesetter output on film or paper, users of these graphical word processors

Illustration programs like CorelDraw allow you to import scanned images.

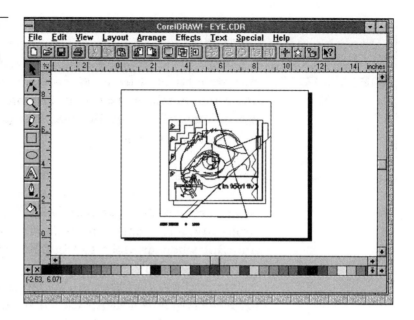

typically produce their pages on a laser or color printer connected directly to their systems. As a result, even though they may appear similar to page layout programs on the surface, there are vast differences in the kinds of documents they can effectively produce. However, keep in mind that documents created in these word processors can always be imported into a page layout program if high-resolution output is needed.

Illustration Programs

Computer graphics come in two varieties: bit-mapped and vector. Bit-mapped graphics—the kind created by scanners—are composed of dots. In contrast, a vector graphic consists of mathematical expressions stored in the computer. These expressions describe various lines, curves, and objects that combine to form graphic images. These images appear on the computer screen as an array of tiny dots. When printed on a laser printer, they also appear as an array of dots. But because they are stored as mathematical expressions, they have several properties that give them advantages over bit-mapped graphics.

An object-oriented graphic, such as the bear's nose, can be enlarged without producing jagged edges.

Vector graphics are resolution-independent. When printed on a 300-dpi laser printer, they can print at 300 dpi. But when printed on a 2400-dpi imagesetter, they print at 2400 dpi. Bit-mapped graphics are essentially locked at a fixed resolution. Vector graphics can also be enlarged or reduced with no loss of image quality. And the objects that compose vector graphics can be reshaped and otherwise modified with tremendous precision.

Vector graphics do a good job of storing and reproducing images that include text, such as corporate logos or trademarks. They are also frequently used to create diagrams, maps, and other line drawings.

Graphics packages that work with vector formats are known as "illustration" programs and include Adobe Illustrator, Macromedia FreeHand, CorelDraw, and Micrografx Designer. CAD programs also use vector graphics.

Instead of offering painting tools, these programs present the user with tools for creating objects. These typically include line tools, curve tools, and tools for creating geometric shapes like circles, ovals, and rectangles. One common feature in these programs is the Bezier curve tool. A Bezier curve is created by placing and manipulating points on the layout. By dragging on "control" points, you can change the shape of the curve. Most illustration programs include a freehand drawing tool that allows you to draw a curve on the screen. Once this is done, the curve is converted to a Bezier and can be reshaped by dragging on the control points.

Once you create an object, you can move it around the screen simply by clicking on it and dragging. You reshape it or resize it by dragging on handles that appear around its edges. You can define the thickness and color of the object's border. You can "fill" the object with a color, pattern, or screen.

Objects created in an illustration program can be used as elements for complex drawings. You can group multiple objects together or place them in front of or behind other objects. Some illustration programs support multiple "layers" on which you can add objects.

Many illustration programs include powerful functions for manipulating text. Once you type text on the screen, you can convert it into a series of lines and curves and then manipulate it as if it were a series of objects. Some programs also include typographic features that allow you to adjust the spacing and width of characters. This makes them suitable for producing flyers, advertisements, and other documents that might otherwise be created with a page layout program.

Most of the better illustration programs have the ability to import bit-mapped images in TIFF, PICT, PCX, or other formats. This allows you to incorporate the image into an illustration as if it were a separate object. In most cases, you can crop or scale the bit-mapped image.

In addition to incorporating bit-mapped images into the illustration, you can also import them as "tracing templates." When you do this, a faded version of the image in the illustration, as if it were "underneath" a piece of tracing paper. You can then use the tools in the illustration program to trace over the bit-mapped image. Many illustration programs also include auto-trace functions that automatically convert bit-mapped images into object-oriented formats. However, they work best with simple black-and-white bit-maps.

The most popular illustration packages for the Macintosh are Macromedia FreeHand and Adobe Illustrator, which are also available in Windows versions. The most popular PC-based illustration package is Corel Draw.

CorelDraw deserves some special mention because it is really a suite of graphic tools and elements centered around a powerful drawing package. As a result, some designers use CorelDraw in much the same way they might use a page layout program. You can import a scanned image, have it duplicated, rotated, or resized, and then combine it with text and other graphics. Once you're done, you can produce the result as four-color separations on an imagesetter. We know of one designer who even uses the program to experiment with different combinations of bit-mapped images. He finds that he can flip, rotate, and re-arrange the bit-mapped elements much faster in CorelDraw than he can with his image-editing software.

Later releases of CorelDraw include a simple image-editing program known as Photo Paint. CorelDraw also comes with an extensive library of typefaces and clip art. Because it supports a wide range of bit-mapped file formats, it can be used as a file conversion program. You can import an image in TIFF or PCX format and then export it in another format.

Presentation Programs

Presentation programs are designed for the creation of slide shows and other presentations. In some ways, they are similar to page layout programs with their ability to integrate text and graphics from a wide range of other

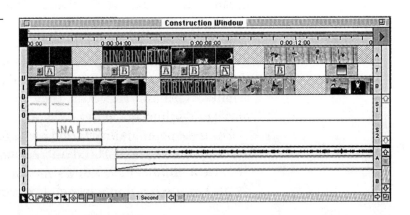

Adobe Premiere lets you import images and filters from Photoshop.

software. However, instead of creating pages, they are used to create frames. These frames can be 35mm slides, overhead transparencies, or screens of information presented directly from the computer. Many of these programs include powerful outlining functions that allow you to structure your presentation as you create the slides. They can also automate the production of speakers' notes.

Most presentation programs can import bit-mapped images in TIFF or other file formats. These images can then be included on slides along with text and other graphic elements. One advantage of presentation programs is that the slides they create use the RGB, instead of the CYMK, color model. We noted earlier that computer monitors do a poor job of displaying images as they will be printed because they use transmissive instead of reflective light. Slides use transmissive light, meaning that you can pretty much tell how the image will appear when you display it on the screen.

Multimedia Programs

Multimedia represents one of the most exciting new developments in the computer business. The term is rather broad-ranging, but generally refers to applications that combine one or more of the following elements: text, computer graphics, animation, sound, and video.

Multimedia projects can take many forms, including CD-ROMs, kiosks, and online services. One of the hottest areas of multimedia is the World Wide Web, which is part of the Internet, that vast telecommunications network that many think is the precursor to the "Information Superhighway." Using what's known as a "Web browser," on your Mac or PC, you can connect to the Web and view "home pages" that include pictures and sound. These pictures can include scanned images.

Multimedia holds great promise as an tool for education and entertainment. One characteristic of multimedia applications is interactivity. This means that the user has control over what information is presented. A multimedia encyclopedia, for example, might offer the option of presenting video clips, sound clips, or animated diagrams of a certain topic. Multimedia also encompasses non-interactive applications, such as hardware and software systems that allow you to create your own videos.

Multimedia titles are often created with what are known as "authoring packages," which in some ways are equivalent to page layout programs in that they are used to combine different elements into a completed project. These elements can include scanned images saved in standard file formats. However, the similarity with page layout software ends there, because professional-level authoring tools generally require a much higher level of user expertise, including the ability to write programs or scripts. In addition to these authoring programs, some presentation packages offer limited multimedia features, allowing you to create on-screen "slide shows" that include animation or sound.

Forms Programs

Another software category that uses scanned images consists of form design programs. These programs are designed for the creation and entry of common business forms like invoices, credit applications, and tax forms. In many ways, they resemble page layout programs, but they offer tools especially designed for adding the kinds of elements found in most business forms.

Forms designers often need to recreate forms that already exist as hard copy. As a result, some forms programs offer functions that allow you to scan a form and import the image into the form layout. You can then use the scanned form as a template for creating an electronic version. These programs can also import bit-mapped or vector images, such as a company logo, for use in the form itself.

CHAPTER 7

Producing the Image

A desktop scanner provides a bridge between real-world images and the digital environment of the microcomputer. Once images have crossed that bridge, they can be retouched, transformed, and incorporated into electronically created documents. But at some point, we need another bridge to bring those documents back into the real world. In other words, our pages, and the scanned images contained within, must be printed.

Prior to the Information Age, the term "printing" was unambiguous. It referred to the process of reproducing pages, usually by means of an offset press. But computers have added a new meaning to the word. In the world of computers, "printing" refers to the process of generating output on a laser printer, color printer, imagesetter, or other output device. In the larger world of graphic communication, the term is expanded to include the process by which the printed output of a computer is used to generate multiple copies of an image.

In this chapter, we'll discuss the many considerations involved in printing scanned images—in both senses of the word. We will discuss the various hardware products that produce output from a computer: laser printers, thermal-transfer printers, inkjet printers, film recorders, imagesetters, and so on. We will see how certain output devices are blurring the distinction between "printing" from a computer and "printing" multiple copies.

Technological advances have a way of changing the way we use language. Because computers have added new meaning to the word "print," users have felt compelled to come up with other terms to distinguish printing in the computer sense from printing in the lithographic sense. To the horror of grammarians who make strict distinctions between nouns and verbs, some computer users like to say that they "output" a page, as if output were an action rather than a thing.

Those poor grammarians have it tough enough keeping up with all the lingo that computer technology has introduced, so we'll make it easy on them. Wherever there is the possibility for confusion, we'll use the term "produce" to describe the process of generating output from a computer system, and "print" to describe the process of reproducing that output on an offset press, color copier, or other printing equipment.

Producing Output

We will begin by discussing the various options for producing output from your computer. These options fall into two general categories.

The first category consists of output that will eventually be reproduced on a copier or press. The output serves as a master, or more technically, a "mechanical," from which copies will be made. The process by which this output is produced is known generally as "prepress," the steps necessary before a job is placed on press.

The second category consists of output that is not intended for reproduction. This includes color comps, proofs, or photographic or fine art originals. You can produce multiple copies from your output device, but those copies will not be used as mechanicals. We can describe this form of printing as "direct digital output" as opposed to prepress.

One important distinction among output devices is whether they produce halftone or continuous-tone output. We first discussed this distinction in Chapter One.

You will recall that a halftone is an image that consists of dots. The dots are relatively large in dark areas and small in light areas. When viewed under normal conditions, the halftone appears much like a normal photograph. The difference is that a halftone can be reproduced in print. A photograph must first be converted to a halftone before it can be printed. Creating halftones is thus a part of prepress. Halftone output devices include laser printers and imagesetters.

We use the terms "screen frequency" or "line screen" to refer to the resolution of a halftone. A halftone printed in a newspaper generally has a screen frequency of 75 to 100 lines per inch. A magazine halftone might have a screen frequency of 133 to 150 lines. High-quality art books or calendars might have a screen frequency of 200 or 300 lines per inch. Halftones with such high screen frequencies are difficult to distinguish from photographs.

In a continuous-tone image, such as a photograph, each dot is a uniform size, but can be a different color or gray tone. In a normal photograph, the "dots" are tiny silver particles, too small to discern even with a magnifying glass. But some digital output devices can also produce continuous-tone images. These might be 300-dpi images, matching the resolution of a laser printer. But because each dot can be a different color, a 300-dpi continuous-tone image looks similar to a halftone printed with a 300-line screen.

Continuous-tone output devices include dye-sublimation printers, Iris inkjet printers, and digital color copiers with PostScript interfaces. Obviously, these are used for direct digital output. But some color printers that are also used for direct output do not have continuous-tone capabilities. These include thermal-transfer printers, most varieties of color inkjet printers, and color laser printers.

There are occasions where continuous-tone output devices are used for prepress work. For example, continuous-tone transparencies produced on a film recorder are often created as a preliminary step to producing color separations. We also know of designers who use continuous-tone prints from Iris Graphics inkjet printers as mechanicals. However, this is the exception that proves the rule. To use this kind of output as a mechanical, it must first be scanned and then color separated on a PostScript imagesetter. Those color separations will consist of halftones.

PostScript

Before we go any further, we need to discuss an important component in most output strategies, a "page description language" known as "PostScript."

PostScript is a programming language with a specialized purpose. Instead of being used to create accounting systems or other computer programs, PostScript is used to instruct a printer or imagesetter how and where to put text and graphics on a page.

Like other programming languages, PostScript uses English-like commands. These commands tell an output device how to place dots on a page. You can theoretically write a PostScript program to create almost any kind of graphic object, but this is rarely practical. Instead, you rely on your graphics software—and a small program known as a PostScript "driver," to create the PostScript program. This program is then copied, or "downloaded," to the output device.

When a printer or imagesetter is said to be "PostScript-compatible," this means it can produce pages created with the PostScript PDL. Within the output device (or a related piece of hardware known as a raster-image processor or RIP) is a PostScript interpreter. The interpreter converts PostScript commands into a format that can be understood by the hardware that actually places the marks on the page.

One advantage of PostScript is device independence. This means that a page or publication produced with a program that supports PostScript can be generated with little or no modification on any PostScript printer or imagesetter. No matter what the resolution of that output device, the page can be produced at the maximum resolution and with the maximum quality.

The original version of PostScript, for all its power, had some limitations in its ability to produce high-quality color images. Some of these problems were transparent to users as hardware and software developers came up with ways to work around them. Adobe added many of its own "fixes"—known as extensions—that made the PDL more capable of producing color. Still, users often found that output devices were very slow when producing complex color PostScript images.

In 1990, Adobe announced PostScript Level 2, a comprehensive upgrade to the PDL. Many of the new features were aimed at color users. It supports several device-independent color spaces based on CIE 1931(XYZ), a standard method for describing color that is based on human visual perception. In theory, the color space acts as a reference point to ensure consistent color output on different printers and imagesetters.

In addition to these color spaces, PostScript Level 2 includes improved algorithms for producing halftones. Some of the improvements apply to all halftones, while others are specific to color images. The general improvements include faster performance and the ability to specify a much wider range of halftone screen angles and frequencies.

Though PostScript is by far the most popular output standard in the desktop publishing market, some alternatives are available. In most cases, these alternatives offer a less expensive option for publishing users who balk at the relatively high cost of PostScript output devices. But as with all low-cost alternatives, there are also trade-offs in terms of quality, performance, convenience, and compatibility.

PostScript's popularity has led a number of companies to develop PostScript-compatible languages, popularly known as PostScript clones. These languages are usually packaged with interpreters and controllers that drive laser printers or imagesetters. In theory, they can interpret all PostScript commands, generating output that is identical to what a true PostScript device would produce.

PostScript clones are sold in several forms. The least expensive are software-only products that can print PostScript files on a non-PostScript printer. They tend to be very slow and usually require some form of extra memory on the computer or in the printer. Other clones are found on controllers installed in the computer or built into the printer itself. Still others are sold as cartridges that plug into the printer.

Output Technologies

Now that we have discussed some of the basic concepts in digital output, we will examine some of the technologies used in output devices.

Laser Printers

Laser printers were the first computer output devices capable of producing high-quality images. Most use a technology similar to that found in office copiers. The core of the machine is a laser "engine." Within the engine, a laser "writes" on a photosensitive drum or belt to create spots that attract toner. The toner then is transferred to paper.

Another important element in the laser printer is the controller, which receives output from the computer system and converts it into instructions that drive the laser. In most PostScript printers, the controller is where the page description software resides. The controller also includes memory, which is used to store an image of the page before it is printed along with any typefaces resident in the printer or downloaded from the computer. In some cases, the controller can also be connected to a hard disk, which is used to store extra typefaces.

In addition to being black-and-white devices, most early laser printers were limited to 300-dpi resolution. This resolution is suitable for producing line art, but is woefully inadequate for producing high-quality halftones.

If a halftone's line screen ranges from 75 to 200 lines per inch, and a laser printer offers 300-dpi resolution, it might

Halftone dots are generated on an imagesetter by grouping together an array of imagesetter dots.

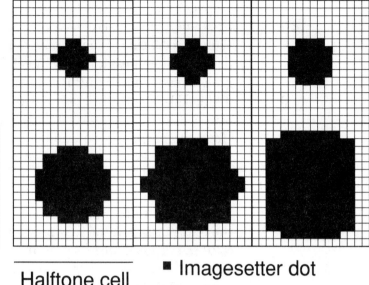

Halftone cell   ▪ Imagesetter dot

seem that a laser printer would be perfectly capable of producing good-looking halftones. However, dots produced by a laser printer are not the same as halftone dots.

To look realistic, a gray-scale image must be capable of reproducing about 256 shades of gray. If you go well below this—say 16 shades of gray—the image will be posterized, with an obvious banding effect in areas of transition between light and dark shades. This means the output device must be capable of producing halftone cells of 256 different sizes. Such a halftone cell would have 16 dots on each side (see diagram), since 16 times 16 equals 256. The size of the cell is determined by the numbers of dots turned "on" or "off" within.

Just as the number of halftone dots per inch determine the halftone's screen frequency, the number of cells per inch determine the line-screen of a digital halftone. With a relatively low-resolution output device like a laser printer, there's a trade-off between screen frequency and the number of gray shades that can be reproduced. If it takes 16 dots on one line to create a 256-dot cell, and you have a 300-dpi laser printer, the number of halftone cells per inch (300 divided by 16) gives you a ridiculously low screen frequency of 18 lines. If you want to increase the screen frequency, you need to reduce the number of gray levels by reducing the size of the cell. If your halftone cell has eight printer dots on each side, you get 64 (8 times 8) possible gray levels and a higher screen frequency of 37 lines (300 divided by 8). If the cell permits 16 levels of gray (four dots on each side), the screen frequency reaches 75 lines. However, none of these trade-offs is very appealing, which is why a 300-dpi laser printer does such a poor job of producing halftones.

Fortunately, laser printer manufacturers have come a long way in improving resolution. Many laser "engines"—the part of the printer that places dots on the page—offer 600-dpi resolution or more. In addition, some manufacturers have figured out a way to "cheat" on the normal resolution of the engine. They use a technique called "laser modulation" to create small variations in the size of laser-printed dots. The result is that a 300-dpi engine can produce output that looks much higher than 300 dpi. And a 600-dpi engine can produce output equivalent to 1200 dpi.

When we get to 1200 dpi, the trade-off between resolution and gray-scale isn't so bad. To create a halftone with 256 shades of gray, you need a halftone cell with 16 dots on each side (16 x 16 equals 256). Divide 1200 by 16 and you get a screen frequency of 75 lines per inch, which is acceptable for many kinds of output.

Printer manufacturers who offer these resolution-enhancement schemes have given their technologies special brand names, sort of like the special ingredients in certain brands of toothpaste. They go by names like "TurboRes" and "FinePrint." Some resolution-enhancement technologies are designed especially for output of halftones. These include LaserMaster's "TurboGray" and Apple's "FotoPrint."

Halftones produced using these techniques are suitable for many applications, such as publications produced on newsprint. Print quality can be enhanced even further if you use one of many grades of paper designed especially for laser printer output. However, to get the best possible halftone quality, you need to produce output on a PostScript imagesetter.

Imagesetters

Before the advent of desktop publishing, almost all publication-quality work was performed on expensive typesetting equipment that produced high-resolution output on a type of paper-like film known as resin-coated (RC) paper. This film would be cut into strips called galleys, which were pasted onto a layout board with hot wax or rubber cement.

These phototypesetters were the forerunners of the output devices known as imagesetters. Imagesetters are capable of producing output at resolutions ranging from 1200 to 3000 dpi on resin-coated paper or clear film. Unlike phototypesetters, which were capable of producing type galleys only, imagesetters can produce output incorporating complete page layouts, including images (hence their name).

The history of the PostScript imagesetter begins in 1986, with Linotype's introduction of the Linotronic 100 and 300 along with the RIP 1. Three years earlier, Linotype had signed an agreement with Adobe Systems giving the PostScript developer rights to use typefaces from the German manufacturer's extensive type library. As part of the deal, Linotype won the right to incorporate the PostScript language into its laser-driven phototypesetters.

Agfa's Accuset is a popular capstan imagesetter.

These products were relatively primitive by current standards, but the basic technology remains the same. A PostScript file is produced with a desktop publishing or graphics package and downloaded from a personal computer to the raster image processor (RIP). Here, the PostScript language commands are converted into an electronic array of tiny dots. This information is passed to the image recorder, where a laser beam exposes the dots onto photosensitive film or paper. The photosensitive medium is then removed from the recorder and sent through a chemical processor, which produces the final output in much the same way a photo processing lab develops your snapshots.

The major limitation in these early imagesetters was the RIP. With its limited memory and speed, Linotype's original RIP 1 had difficulty handling complex pages, especially those that included halftones or other images. Subsequent RIPs have steadily improved in performance and imaging capabilities.

Due to their limitations, early imagesetters were suitable mainly for producing type, line art, and black-and-white halftones. Though some hardy pioneers experimented with producing color separations on these machines, output quality was suspect.

Leading manufacturers of PostScript imagesetters include Linotype-Hell, Agfa, Scitex, Optronics, Screen, and DuPont/Crosfield. Linotype-Hell, Agfa, and Scitex are the market leaders.

Color Separations

When an imagesetter produces color separations, it does not produce film or paper in color. Instead, it produces four pieces of film containing a negative of the image. Each piece of film is used to create a plate, one for cyan ink, the second for yellow, the third for magenta, and the fourth for black. These plates are mounted on a four-color printing press. As paper runs through the press, each of the four process color inks are applied in succession. The CYMK colors combine to create what looks like a full-color image.

To produce a good-looking color image, the imagesetter must be capable of generating separations with a high degree of dot "repeatability." This means that the dots must be positioned on each plate with a high degree of precision. Otherwise, the output will suffer from misregistration and moire patterns. You can see this sometimes in color images printed in newspapers. If one of the plates is out of register, the process ink is offset by a slight amount, and all of the colors are somewhat distorted.

In addition to their slow RIPs, early imagesetters designed for monochrome output often suffered from poor repeatability. One culprit was the feeding mechanism used to pull the paper or film media through the image recorder. Most early imagesetters used a roller feed (also known as "capstan") mechanism that lacked the ability to precisely align dots from one separation to another. The problem was compounded by the way film or paper was imaged: instead of imaging the entire page at once, the rollers pulled the media in a constant stop-start motion that also affected repeatability.

Imagesetter manufacturers have since developed capstan mechanisms that offer much improved repeatability. But the best repeatability—and the best color separation output in general—comes from imagesetters that use drum-based mechanisms. Film is mounted on a drum that rotates inside the imagesetter. As the drum rotates, a laser beam etches dots onto the film.

In addition to producing process color separations, most imagesetters—even older ones—are capable of producing spot color separations. Spot color differs from process color in that the press applies ink in the extra color rather combining CYMK inks. It is generally used when only one or two extra colors are needed. For example, you may have a page in which you want a line drawing to appear in red and text to appear in black. You create two separations, one with the text, the other with the line drawing. The plate created from the text separation applies black ink, while the other plate applies black ink.

Sometime spot and process color separations might be combined. Instead of producing four separations, you might produce five: one for the CYMK colors, and one for an additional spot color. The spot color separation might be used to apply a color not easily reproduced with CYMK. Common examples are metallic colors like gold and silver, or fluorescent colors.

Using two color separations, you can get an interesting halftone effect known as a duotone. A duotone is created by combining two copies of the same halftone. One copy is in black-and-white, while the other is in an extra color, usually shaded to some degree. The halftone dot angles in the two images are different so that the dots don't lay on top of one another. Double-black duotones, in which both overlays are black, render images with richer dark shades than would be seen in a simple black-and-white halftone.

Screening

One of the most important features in an imagesetter is it screening capability, that is, the range of functions it has for producing halftones. Because this is such an important consideration for working with scanned images, screening technology deserves some detailed discussion here.

We've already discussed the method by which we measure the resolution of a halftone: its "line screen" or "screen frequency," measured in lines per inch. Two other variables that affect the appearance of halftones are the screen angle and dot shape.

To envision the concept of screen angle, imagine a piece of graph paper in which the intersection of each line represents the center of each halftone dot. The dots are thus arranged in neat horizontal and vertical rows. The problem is that halftones created in this way are not visually pleasing. To create a more effective optical illusion, most black-and-white halftones are printed with a 45-degree screen angle. Using the 45-degree angle has the effect of better hiding the dot pattern. To visualize this, take your graph paper and turn it so that the lines between each dot run diagonally instead of vertically and horizontally.

Dots in a halftone can be one of many shapes. The most common are round, square, and elliptical, but other shapes can be used as well. Each shape has advantages and disadvantages that depend in part on the kind of image to be reproduced. For example, round dots are better than square dots in reproducing fleshtones. Square dots are better suited in images with fine details. Elliptical dots are best for high screen frequencies or images that include a variety of subjects.

So far, we have discussed screening as it applies to black-and-white images. Color halftones have similar

Stochastic, or frequency-modulated screening, is a new technique for producing screened images on an imagesetter. In traditional AM screening, the size of the dots vary while the spacing is consistent. In FM screening, the size is consistent but the spacing varies.

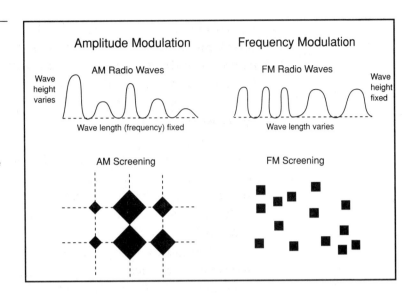

characteristics, except that everything is multiplied by four. In addition to black ink, we use cyan, magenta, and yellow.

During prepress operations, an imagesetter is used to produce four separations, one for each process color. The dots in each separation are printed at different angles, generally 15 degrees for cyan, 45 degrees for black, 75 degrees for magenta, and 90 degrees for yellow. The pattern of CYMK dots formed by these angles is known as a "rosette."

Before the dawn of digital imaging, traditional halftones were created with a photographic process. A continuous-tone image was photographed through a halftone screen, converting it into a series of variable-sized dots. Digital imaging systems use software to perform essentially the same function. This software is generally located in the imagesetter RIP. Each company that manufactures RIPs also offers its own selection of screening technologies to create halftones.

Like the laser printer, an imagesetter produces halftones in the form of cells that are equivalent to a halftone dot. Because imagesetter resolutions generally range from about 1000 dots per inch to 4000 dpi or more, they can build halftone cells that are small enough to produce images with screen frequencies of 100 lines or more. For example, with a 1200-dpi imagesetter and a 256-gray-level halftone cell (16 dots per side), you get a maximum screen frequency of 75 lines (1200 divided by 16). A 2400-dpi imagesetter gives you a maximum line screen of 150 lines (2400 divided by 16).

However, this assumes that your halftones are printed at a 90-degree angle. As noted above, a gray-scale image looks best when printed at a 45-degree screen angle. When you rotate the dots, the math starts to get very complicated, and higher resolution becomes even more important. Things get even more complicated when we talk about color, because as noted above, each color separation must be printed at specific screen angles (15 degrees cyan, 45 degrees black, 75 degrees magenta, 90 degrees yellow).

Whatever its resolution—1200 dpi, 2400 dpi, or 4000 dpi—each imagesetter prints dots in a fixed grid. The challenge for digital screening technologies is to create halftone cells that replicate as closely as possible traditional dot shapes and screen angles while fitting into this grid. Numerous vendors, including Adobe, Agfa, Linotype-Hell, and Scitex, have created screening algorithms that attempt to meet this challenge in various ways.

Most of these screening technologies fall into two general categories, "rational" and "irrational" tangent screening. The terms "rational" and "irrational" refer to the kinds of mathematical calculations needed to compute which dots the imagesetter turns "on" or "off" when producing halftone cells.

In a nutshell, rational tangent technologies offer a relatively limited choice of screen angles that approximate those used in traditional color halftones without matching them exactly. Older rational tangent technologies, such as Linotype-Hell's RT Screening, were especially limited in the choice of screen angles. Newer "supercell" technologies, which combine halftone cells produced by the imagesetter into larger "supercells," can better approximate traditional screen angles. Examples include Linotype-Hell's HQS Screening, Agfa's Balanced Screening, and Adobe's Accurate Screens.

Irrational tangent screening technologies, such as Linotype-Hell's IS Technology, offer a wider choice of screen angles and frequencies, coming even closer to matching traditional angles. The downside is that the screening algorithms require lots of calculations, thus calling for a powerful processor in the RIP.

Stochastic Screening

The screening technologies described so far attempt to duplicate as closely as possible the angles, dot shapes, and frequencies used to produce traditional halftones. However, numerous vendors have unveiled a new technology called "stochastic" or "frequency-modulated" screening that introduces an entirely new model for reproducing images on press.

Rather than providing a digital equivalent of a traditional halftone with variable-sized dots, stochastic screening uses much smaller dots of a uniform size that are randomly spaced. The dot patterns we see in traditional halftones essentially vanish, and the images appear to be nearly continuous tone. Examples of stochastic screening technologies include Linotype-Hell's Diamond Screening and Agfa's Cristal Raster.

One advantage of stochastic screening is that it eliminates certain kinds of moiré patterns. In Chapter Four, we described what happens when you try to scan an image that has already been printed as a halftone. When the image is printed, the two halftone screens conflict with each other and you get an unsightly grid-like effect called a moiré pattern. Stochastic screening helps prevent another kind of moiré, one that arises from the image itself. For example, if a photograph includes textiles or other subjects with regularly occuring patterns, they can create interference with the screen pattern in the halftone. However, because a stochastic image has no regular pattern of dots, the interference is eliminated.

Stochastic screening is also highly amenable to emerging high-fidelity color printing technologies, which use a six-, seven-, or eight-color process instead of conventional four-color process. High-fidelity printing offers richer color reproduction and a wider range of printable colors than four-color process, but also taxes the capabilities of conventional screening techniques because of the extra dots. Because stochastic screening does not force dots into a fixed pattern, it can accommodate extra process colors more easily than most conventional screening technologies.

Some printing industry experts believe stochastic screening will revolutionize the graphic arts market. However, the technology poses some challenges for commercial printers, some of whom will have to change their normal printing procedures to accommodate the technology. It is too early to tell just what impact stochastic screening will have, but within a few years it is likely that many graphic artists will turn to stochastic screening for production of high-quality images.

Impositions

In addition to capstan and drum mechanisms, imagesetters are distinguished by their maximum image area. Imagesetters with especially large image areas are capable of producing complete impositions. An imposition is a large form that includes multiple pages—anywhere from four to 32. A plate made from the imposition is used on a large sheetfed or web press to print signatures. These signatures are then folded and cut to create the finished publication. Signatures are generally used in the printing of newspapers, magazines, books, and other publications containing many pages.

Platesetters

The imagesetters discussed in this chapter produce output on film. But there is another kind of imagesetter, called a platesetter, that produces output directly on printing plates. Instead of creating film and then using a platemaking machine, the printer can simply create the plates directly from digital files and mount them on press.

For years, manufacturers of imagesetter media like 3M and Mitsubishi have offered plate materials that work with standard imagesetters. However, these materials had serious limitations. They could not be used for four-color work, and lacked the durability needed for press runs beyond 10,000 or so.

The new generation of platesetters from companies like Creo and Gerber produce color separation output on standard aluminum plates used in the printing industry. In 1995, *Scientific American* used a platesetter to produce an entire special edition on computer applications.

Another new technology employs "dry film" instead of the traditional graphic arts films used with imagesetters. Traditional film processing is a messy affair with all kinds of environmental consequences, including silver byproducts that must be disposed of in a safe manner. Dry film is processed using some combination of heat, light, and/or electricity, eliminating the need for traditional chemical processing.

Proofing

In the section that follows, we will discuss color output devices, some of which can be used to produce digital color proofs. But it's also important that we cover the kind of proofing that's still favored in the printing industry, the traditional film-based or halftone proof.

First let's discuss just what we mean by a "proof." In the days before digital technology, "proof" had a specific meaning: it was a way of closely approximating how a color image would look when printed. If it was a true "contract proof," it provided a benchmark for the commercial printer. Once you signed off on the proof, the printer used it as a reference for the press run. If the final printed piece seriously deviated from the proof, it was the printer and not the customer who had to make good on the job. Today, the meaning of "proof" has expanded to include a variety of technologies that may or may not accurately predict the final look of a job.

Short of an actual press proof—a sample produced on press—traditional halftone proofs are the most accurate way to predict how a color image will look in print. These proofs are created directly from the film that will be used to make plates. Most can be produced on a variety of substrates simulating commonly used paper stocks, and can reveal moiré patterns, poor color balance, and other conditions that affect print quality. Most use pigments that conform to the SWOP (Specifications for Web Offset Printing) standard used in the North American printing industry. Leading vendors include DuPont, Kodak, 3M, Hoechst-Celanese, Fuji, and Agfa.

The first popular off-press proofing system was DuPont's Cromalin, which was introduced in the 1960s but remains in use today. Other popular systems include 3M Matchprint, Hoechst-Celanese Pressmatch, Fuji Color-Art, Agfa's AgfaProof, and DuPont's WaterProof. These are all known as "laminate systems," meaning the films or color layers in the proof are all fused together. However, some vendors also offer overlay proofing systems in which color film corresponding to each separation is taped to a backing sheet. These are not as accurate as laminate systems, but can be used to check spot colors or tints. They are also less costly than laminate proofs.

These systems are highly accurate in predicting color, but they still require that you first create film on an imagesetter. If you are going directly to a digital printing device, such as one of the new digital presses, these film proofs won't do you any good at all. This has led some manufacturers to develop proofing systems that work directly with digital files. Unlike most color printers, these systems attempt to duplicate as closely as possible the halftone dots that will appear when the piece is printed. Products in this category include Kodak's Approval system and Optronics' IntelliProof. IntelliProof is essentially an imagesetter with built-in proofing features.

Color Output Devices

So far, we have discussed output devices aimed at prepress applications. But many color printers can be used to produce direct color output. They are used in the following applications:

To create "comprehensives" or "comps." A comp is a mock-up of a printing job that a designer shows a client for approval purposes. If the client likes the comp, the designer goes on with the project. If the client doesn't like the comp, the designer comes up with a new design and tries again.

To create print proofs. A proof, as opposed to a comp, is a color print designed to predict how a job will look when it is finally printed. The problem with most color output devices is that they don't always do a good job of imitating the output of a printing press. Color printers are often used to create preliminary proofs that give you a rough prediction of how the job will look. For a more exact prediction, you need a "film proof." This is a color print generated directly from the film produced on an imagesetter.

To create fine art or photographic originals. If you are a fine artist or photographer, you probably don't need many copies of your work. In this case, you can use a color printer to produce the desired number of copies directly.

To create transparencies. Using a film recorder, you can create high-quality 35mm slides or 4x5 transparencies. Slides can be used for slide presentations or as a convenient way of archiving images. Transparencies are often used as a preliminary step before the production of color separations. The advantage of transparencies is that a single piece of film can be used to produce a wide variety of output, from a small ad to a large poster or billboard. Many advertising agencies use transparency output for product shots.

Thermal-Transfer Printers

Thermal-transfer printers are among the least-expensive options for producing direct color output. In a thermal-transfer engine, a print head melts tiny dots of plastic or wax into the paper. The plastic or wax is stored on sheets or ribbons, contained in a cartridge, that scroll through the printer in much the same way that film moves through a camera. Most cartridges come in one of two varieties: three-color and four-color. The three-color cartridges use cyan, yellow, and magenta as their primary colors, while the four-color versions add black. Cyan, yellow, and magenta can be combined to create black, but the printers generally get better results using all four primary colors, especially when producing text output in black ink.

Thermal wax-transfer printers can do an adequate job of producing color pages, but they have some limitations. Photographic images produced on these printers tend to have a grainy, dithered appearance that results from the way dots are laid on the page. As a result, these printers do a poor job of predicting how a color print job will look on press. In addition, they are limited in the kinds of media they can handle. They generally require thermal paper or transparency film for best printing results.

As inkjet printers have fallen in price, some vendors are positioning thermal-transfer printers for one area where inkjets fall short: producing transparencies for overhead projectors.

Inkjet Printers

In an inkjet printer, ink in three or four of the primary colors is sprayed through tiny nozzles on to the page. These printers are slow, but are also inexpensive (under $1000) and offer excellent image quality for the price. Another advantage is that they can print on plain paper. Examples of these printers include the Epson Stylus and Hewlett-Packard DeskJet.

One variation on the inkjet printer uses solid inks that resemble crayons instead of the liquid inks used in the Stylus or DeskJet. The ink melts almost instantly at a certain temperature, but solidifies just as quickly slightly below that temperature. When sprayed on the page, the

Scanning for Large-Format Output

APPLICATION BRIEF

When scanning images for output on an inkjet or electrostatic plotter, many users make the mistake of scanning images with too much resolution. Because the image will probably be considerably enlarged, it is tempting to scan it with as much resolution as possible—even if the files produced in this manner become unmanageably large. Other users make the opposite mistake and scan with not enough resolution. To strike a happy medium, calculate the percentage by which the image will be enlarged and then multiply this by a number between 60 and 100. Use the higher end of the range if image sharpness is important and the lower end if it's more important to keep file size down. Suppose the original is an 8 x 10-inch print that will be enlarged to 24 x 30 inches, or 300 percent. We thus scan the image at 180 to 300 dpi (60 x 3 = 180; 100 x 3 = 300). Keep in mind that this is a rule of thumb, and every large-format output system is different. Always discuss the job with your imaging service before you begin to get their advice on the best settings to use when scanning for large-format output.

ink dries before it can be absorbed, most of it remaining on the surface of the paper.

One limitation of solid-ink technology is that it does not do a good job of printing on transparencies. Solid inks tend to have a "beaded" texture that distorts light passing through the medium.

Dye Transfer Printers

Dye transfer, also known as dye-sublimation technology, is a variation on thermal-transfer technology. A thermal print head transfers dye from a ribbon to the paper or film on which the image is to be printed. Unlike conventional

Dye sublimation printers can produce photographic-quality color output.

thermal-transfer printers, which melt tiny dots of wax or plastic onto the page, dye-sublimation printers can vary the intensity of each dot. This makes it possible to produce continuous-tone images. However, the technology is limited to printing on transparency film or a special kind of thermal paper.

Dye transfer printers used to be very expensive, but have come down considerably in price. They are a favorite of photographers and fine artists because their output looks almost indistinguishable from a quality color photograph.

Some vendors offer printers that combine dye-sublimation and thermal-transfer printing technologies. If dye-sublimation output is so much better than thermal-transfer output, you may wonder why someone would want to combine these technologies, but it all boils down to economics. The "consumables"—paper and ink—in a thermal-transfer printer are much less costly than the consumables for a dye-sublimation printer. A designer using one of these hybrid machines can produce preliminary prints of a job using thermal-transfer output then switch to dye-sub for the final print that will be shown to a client.

3M offers a dye sublimation printer called the Rainbow that it has targeted at the graphic arts market. One use of the Rainbow is as a preliminary proofing device. It will not predict the look of a printed piece as well as a film proof, but has the advantage of producing output directly from digital files and is considerably less expensive on a per-print basis.

Color Copiers

Another important printing trend in recent years is the digital color copier. These products, which include Canon's CLC series and the Xerox Majestik, can produce color copies just like a standard photocopier produces black-and-white prints. However, they also feature digital interfaces, which means they can be connected to a computer system.

Several companies offer interface products that permit computer output on a digital color copier. In addition to the actual interface, these products include PostScript (or PostScript clone) interpreters, extra memory, and software that automatically color-corrects images to produce high-quality output. The best of these products allow the color copier to produce continuous-tone image similar to what a dye-sublimation printer can produce.

The most popular of these products is the Fiery controller from Electronics for Imaging (EFI). The controller is so popular, in fact, that prints produced from a Fiery-equipped copier (and some produced with competing products) are often known as "Fiery" prints. Numerous other vendors offer controllers for digital color copiers as well.

Color copiers—and interface products like the Fiery—are very expensive. However, many service bureaus offer output on Canon CLC copiers with the Fiery controller or one of its competitors.

One interesting application for these copiers is T-shirt transfers. By producing output on special transfer materials instead of paper, you can convert your digital images into a form that can be worn on your back. However, this is a tricky process, and not all service bureaus offer it.

Colorbus, which develops a print controller called the Cyclone that competes with the Fiery, also offers a product called CopiPress that allows you to transfer images produced on the color copier to binders and other solid objects.

Iris Printers

Iris Graphics, a Scitex subsidiary based in Massachusetts, offers a series of continuous-tone inkjet printers used by service bureaus, some of which specialize in fine arts or photographic output. The printers are expensive, with price tags of $30,000 or more depending on the maximum image size and other factors. But they have become popular for high-end imaging applications.

In addition to producing photorealistic output, the Iris printers can work with a wide variety of substrates (paper surfaces). This is an advantage over dye-transfer printers, which are more limited in the substrates they support. One Iris model, the 3047, is capable of producing output up to 32 x 47 inches.

Large-Format Output

One of the fastest-growing areas in the digital imaging market is large-format output, loosely defined as anything bigger than tabloid size (11 x 17 inches). This capability is provided by inkjet or electrostatic plotters in combination with PostScript-compatible "front-end" systems. These plotters can produce output ranging up to 52 inches by 30 feet at resolutions ranging from 200 to 400 dpi.

Large-format output systems are used in a wide range of applications, including trade show signage, retail point-of-sale displays, shopping mall signage, courtroom displays, and business presentations. Some of these systems can even be used to produce outdoor billboards, adhesive signage for vehicles, and floor decals for retail establishments.

Electrostatic plotters operate in a manner similar to color copiers, applying toners in the CYMK process colors. They are expensive, with prices beginning at $40,000 or so, but also fast. As a result, they tend to be favored by productivity-minded service bureaus. The leading manufacturer of electrostatic plotters is Xerox ColorGrafX, which offers models with 42- and 52-inch image widths. Inkjet plotters are typically much slower, but are also priced at less than $10,000. Leading models include Encad's NovaJet and Hewlett-Packard's DesignJet 650C, both of which offer 300-dpi resolution and a maximum width of 36 inches.

Electrostatic and inkjet plotters both print on roll-fed paper, meaning that the output can be nearly any length. In most cases, the output is laminated and mounted on foam or core board to improve durability.

One of the most important components in a large-format system is the front-end, which provides the digital link to the plotter in much the same way a RIP drives an

LaserMaster's
Displaymaker Express
is a large-format color
inkjet plotter.

imagesetter. While only a handful of companies manufacture plotters, many vendors offer front-end systems that work with electrostatic and/or inkjet plotters. They include Cactus, Colossal Graphics, LaserMaster, Management Graphics, and Visual Edge Technology.

In some cases, these front-end systems will play a bigger role in determining image quality than the plotter itself. For example, each vendor offers their own form of screening. Most use a screening technique called error diffusion that is similar to the stochastic screening techniques described earlier in this chapter. If you look up close at a large-format print, you will see that it consists of tiny, randomly spaced dots rather than larger halftone dots.

In 1995, LaserMaster Corp. introduced the first 54-inch inkjet plotter, called the DisplayMaker Express. This product, which rivals electrostatic plotters in terms of speed and quality, uses disks of solid ink. Some service providers who rejected the first generation of inkjet plotters based on Hewlett-Packard and Encad engines because of their slow speed are turning to the DisplayMaker Express because of its drastically improved performance.

Film Recorders

Film recorders are used to record computer images directly on photographic film. In most cases, the film must be processed at a photo lab. Depending on the resolution of the film recording process, film recorders can produce transparencies ranging from 35 mm slides to 8x10s.

Film recorders have numerous uses. You can produce 35mm slides for business presentations or to distribute product photographs to trade publications or other media.

In Hollywood, some imaging services produce transparencies of movie ads and video packages as a preliminary step in the prepress process. One advantage is that the same transparency that eventually produces an ad in a newspaper can also be enlarged into a poster or billboard.

Some digital photo labs also use film recorders as an alternative to the large-format output devices described earlier in this chapter. A digital file is produced on the film recorder as an 8x10 transparency and then enlarged using traditional photographic techniques.

Unlike other output devices, film recorders measure resolution in terms of total lines. An image produced at 2K resolution has a total of 2000 lines. Other common resolution options are 4K and 8K. In general, the larger the transparency, the higher the resolution needed.

We noted earlier that you may get an unpleasant surprise if you assume that the image on an RGB monitor will look the same when it's printed on a CYMK output device. However, another unique aspect of film recorders is that they use an RGB color space instead of CYMK. This makes the designer's life much easier, because the images on the slides will more closely match the images displayed on the monitor.

Some film recorders are capable of producing direct output on film, meaning you don't have to get it processed. These include the Fire 1000 from Cymbolic Sciences International and the Kodak LVT.

CD Recorders

For most of this chapter, we have focused on output devices that produce prints or film. But there is another kind of output device that's becoming popular these days, even though you might not think of it as one. We're talking about compact disc recorders, products that allow you to create what are essentially your own CD-ROMs.

In technical terms, the CDs created by these systems are not CD-ROMs. The "ROM" in that familiar acronym stands for "read-only memory," meaning that you can read data from the disc, but you can't record anything on it.

A CD recorder allows you to store data on a recordable CD.

However, discs created by a CD recording system can be used with any standard CD-ROM drive. Most of these systems can also be used to create your own audio CDs.

As a computer medium, CDs have several advantages. They are relatively inexpensive, they can store huge amounts of data (between 600 and 700 megabytes per disc), and there is a huge base of computer users who have CD-ROM drives capable of accepting the discs.

For users of desktop scanners, CDs can serve double-duty as publishing and archiving media. For example, photographers can scan their best shots and record them to a CD to create an electronic portfolio or stock photo collection. This is an especially popular application for Kodak's Photo CD technology. If you're a multimedia producer, you can use a CD recorder to create prototypes of your interactive titles before they are mass-replicated.

On the archiving side, CD recorders allow you to store large numbers of images on a disc. Because it is a read-only medium, the images cannot be accidentally erased, as they could with tape or magnetic disk backup. In addition, data stored on magnetic disk or tape has a tendency to decay over time due to limitations in the storage medium. By contrast, the data on a CD has a projected lifetime of at least several decades.

The first CD recorders were priced well over $10,000. However, prices have plummeted, and CD recording systems can be had for less than $2000. Early systems were also slow, requiring as much time to record the disc as it does to play it. Newer multispeed CD recorders allow you to record a disc at two, four, or six times the playback speed. A 2X system, for example, records at twice the playback rate.

These CD recorders are not appropriate for creating mass quantities of CDs. In addition to their relatively slow speed—even a 6X drive takes about 10 minutes to create a disc—the CDs that work with these drives are much more expensive than standard discs. However, if you do want to create your own mass-market CD-ROM titles, you can use your recordable CD as a "preliminary master." CD mastering facilities—the places that produce audio CDs and CD-ROMs for the masses—can use the disc as a starting point in the replication process.

CHAPTER 8

Working with an Imaging Service

In the last chapter, we discussed some of the issues involved with producing an image that has been captured on a color scanner. As you can see, in many cases this means a visit to an digital imaging service equipped with the high-priced hardware needed to produce good-looking images.

In some ways, imaging firms are sort of like restaurants. Each has a menu of services from which you can choose: high-resolution drum scanning, imagesetter output, film recorder output, Kodak Photo CD production, commercial printing, and so on. Some offer a broad selection of these services, while others specialize in one or two.

Some of the principal categories of imaging services include:

Digital prepress. When many people think of "service bureaus," this is the kind of company that often comes to mind. Typically, they specialize in producing color separation films for offset lithography using PostScript imagesetters. Most of these services also offer scanning, digital color proofing (such as from 3M's Rainbow, described in Chapter Seven), and traditional color proofing.

Digital printing. These companies allow you to produce output on high-speed printing devices that work directly with digital files. Instead of producing film, making plates, and mounting them on a press, you can have the entire job produced in one step from a PostScript file. Some of the technologies you might find here include digital color copiers (such as the Canon CLC series), high-speed laser printing systems (e.g. Xerox DocuTech), large-format output systems (e.g. Encad's NovaJet), or one of the new digital presses from Indigo, Xeikon, or other vendors. This category would also include services that use Iris Graphics inkjet printers to produce high-quality output of digital fine art or photography.

Reprographics firms. These companies got their start offering CAD plotting services to architects and engineers. However, many now offer large-format output on electrostatic or inkjet plotters as well as prints from the Canon CLC or other digital copiers.

Photo labs. Many companies that serve the needs of professional photographers have added digital imaging divisions geared toward that clientele. Typical services include slide or transparency output, continuous-tone output on dye-sublimation or inkjet printers, and Photo CD processing.

Transparency services. These companies specialize in production of slides and transparencies. Many also offer photo retouching and compositing services. Some of these companies are geared toward the presentation market and can help you set up complete slide presentations. Others are more oriented toward the prepress market, serving ad agencies and others that need high-quality transparencies of product shots or print ads.

CD-ROM services. These firms specialize in production of CD-ROMs. One major subcategory is the Photo CD processor, which can convert a roll of film into a compact disc containing images in Eastman Kodak's Photo CD format.

Quick printers. You may not have thought of it, but your neighborhood quick printer might also be considered a digital imaging facility. Most quick printers these days have Macintosh- or PC-based desktop publishing systems with laser printers, but some also have imagesetters, scanners, large-format systems, and other digital imaging equipment.

Scan Textured Line Art as a Photo

APPLICATION BRIEF   *Normally, when you're scanning a piece of line art like a drawing or diagram, you want to scan in line-art mode to get a crisp, clean image. But some line drawings have textured areas like screens and patterns in them. These can be difficult to capture in line-art mode. As an alternative, scan the entire diagram as a photo. Then, once you've brought it into your image-editing program, you can select the patterned areas and perform image-editing manipulations on them. Sometimes, the simple brightness and constrast controls can be tweaked to optimize the appearance of a patterned area on a line drawing. After you have group-selected the patterned areas on the page, perform an inverse selection to select only the true line-art portions of the drawing. Then use the levels or threshold function to convert these areas to line-art (one-bit-per-pixel). Notice that line-art portions can exist within a gray-scale or 24-bit color image.*

Commercial printers. Commercial printers are the workhorses of the printing industry, producing most of the books, magazines, advertising brochures, and other printed material that we read. Many commercial printers have added electronic prepress departments that produce color separations, and eventually plates, for their offset presses. The customer simply hands over a disk and gets back the final printed product.

Multimedia producers. These companies specialize in helping you produce interactive multimedia titles, digital video, and other forms of "new media."

Obviously, there is much overlap among many of these services. Multimedia producers, for example, are likely to offer CD-ROM services. Many digital prepress facilities and commercial printers have installed digital presses.

And some photo labs have installed large-format systems even though they do not produce continuous-tone output.

You can locate an imaging service bureau by looking for their advertisements in local computer and graphics publications. Trade associations such as the Printing Industry of America can also make recommendations of their members in your area. And manufacturers of graphic arts products can also point you in the right direction.

One challenge in dealing with imaging firms is figuring out which tasks to perform in-house and which to send out to the service bureau. This is especially true when it comes to scanners. If you are reading this book, you probably have your own scanner or are thinking of buying one. But there may be times when you need the image quality that can only be provided by a drum scanner at your local service bureau.

Also keep in mind that a single project may require a visit to multiple imaging services. Conceivably, you could use one service for scanning, another for color separation output, a commercial printer to reproduce the job, and even a large-format service to produce poster-sized prints of the job for a trade show display.

Service bureaus can be valuable allies in your quest to get good-looking images. In many areas, especially large cities, there is a lot of competition among service bureaus, and they will do everything they can to keep you happy. They will offer you advice and work with you to help you create the best-looking output possible.

Buying Out Scans

Even when you've found what seems to be the perfect color scanner for your price and quality requirements, there will still be times when you need to buy out scans from a scanning service. The most likely scenario is a project involving a color photograph that must be printed at a large size or very high line screen. For example, a full-page magazine cover reproduced at 200 lines per inch could require a file size over 45 megabytes. Even if your in-house scanner has sufficient resolution to produce a file this large, you may want to send that scan out anyway, especially if the same prepress house will be producing your film. Most likely, they have a file management system that lets them manipulate and transfer that file more easily than you can in-house.

Here are some other reasons why you might want to send out for scans:

Your original image has subtle details over a wide tonal range. Although many desktop scanners have a density range of 3.0 or more, you may find that a high-end drum scanner will do a better job of capturing details in both the shadows and highlights, particularly if a trained operator is tweaking the controls.

Your original is physically larger than your scanner can accommodate. Blueprints, posters, charts, and 8 x 10 transparencies may fall in this category. While it is possible to scan a large image in swaths and then reassemble the swaths with your image-editing software, sometimes, that's more trouble than it's worth.

You're in a time crunch. If you have many images to scan in a short time, they all need some form of correction or manipulation, and you're short on staff, why give yourself a heart attack? Most imaging service bureaus offer discounts on scanning a large number of images, or they might be willing to eat the rush charges if you make it worth their while, especially if they are producing your film.

OPI Servers

If you do buy out your scans, you may want to take advantage of a technology called OPI that makes working with scanned images much easier. OPI, which stands for Open Prepress Interface, is a prepress industry standard that allows users and vendors of PostScript imaging services to communicate information about images without actually having to include the image data itself.

In a typical scenario, OPI works like this:

1. Before you begin the process of creating a page layout, you send all prints, slides, and transparencies that must be scanned to your service bureau.

2. The service bureau scans the prints, slides, and transparencies on a high-resolution drum scanner and stores them on an OPI print server. Because the images are scanned at high resolution, the files are very large, consuming dozens or even hundreds of megabytes.

3. Software on the server generates a low-resolution version of each image that consumes a fraction of the file size of the original. These files are copied to a disk and sent back to the customer.

4. The customer places the low-resolution images in the page layout. The images can be moved, scaled, and cropped, but cannot be retouched or modified in any other manner. Because the images are so much smaller (in terms of file size) than the originals, they can be placed on the page without causing serious performance bottlenecks. These images are known as "placeholders" or "FPOs" (for position only).

5. The customer completes the job and sends it to the service bureau, which places it on the print server. When the job is printed, the OPI software automatically replaces

Adobe Color Central is an OPI image server.

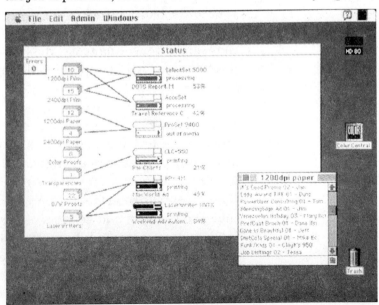

Use Positioning to Scan Oversize Documents

APPLICATION BRIEF

Oversize documents, such as newspapers and posters, can present a challenge to scanner users. The only way to scan oversize documents (short of reducing them first on a photocopier or camera) is to scan them in tiles. If you select the location of the tiles carefully, you'll make it easier to stitch them back together in your image editing program. First, make sure the original lies flat and straight on your flatbed scanner. If necessary, use tape or weights to make sure it doesn't move. Try aligning the corner of the document to the corner of the scanner bed to make this easier. Capture as much as you can on the first scan, and then move the document over to capture the next swath. In general, try to move the original in only one dimension at a time. Name you files appropriately so that you can reassemble them easily; for example: Photo 1A, 2A, 1B, 2B. Once you've set your scanner settings such as resolution, scale factor, and image controls for the first scan, make sure you keep these settings the same for subsequent scans. When you're done scanning, bring each of the tiles into your image-editing program. Create a new file whose canvas is large enough to accomadate all of the pieces of the image. Copy and paste the images into position using the arrow keys if necessary to nudge the tiles into precise position. You may also want to experiment with the Paste Behind function in Photoshop to protect the image already in place from the new image being pasted.

the low-resolution placeholder with the high-resolution original, cropping or scaling as necessary.

The advantages of this strategy should be easy to see. Using the placeholder image instead of the original speeds production and eases the transport of files to and from your service bureau. In addition, you leave the most difficult prepress responsibilities, such as scanning and color correction, to people who have high-end scanners and extensive experience.

On the other hand, OPI limits the special effects you can perform. In general, you can't take advantage of photo manipulation functions such as image merging, silhouetting, or special filters.

Output Options

Hardware manufacturers have given us many options for producing output of scanned images. The options you choose depend in large part on what you plan to do with the job. One nice thing about digital images is that you can get multiple uses from them. The flyer you produced as film on an imagesetter can be easily modified into a point-of-purchase display printed on a large-format plotter.

In a typical scenario, you might begin by producing a color "comp" to give a client an idea of how a job will look when it is finished. When you are ready to take your job to a service bureau, you may want to generate a digital "proof" to check for errors. At the service bureau, your file will be "ripped" and produced as color separations on an imagesetter. You will then take those separations to a commercial printer, who will turn them into plates for offset lithography and eventually into finished pages.

Or perhaps you are a photographer or fine artist who needs just a few copies of your work. Rather than preparing your files for color separation output, you want to produce them directly on a color output device: a dye-sublimation printer, an inkjet printer, perhaps a digital color copier. You can produce your output in quantities of one, 10, 20, or even 100.

Then again, maybe you want to experiment with one of the new digital color presses, such as Heidelberg's GTO-DI or Indigo's E-Print. Here, the press acts as if it were a color printer. You (or more likely your imaging service) send your output to the press over a local-area network. The press then prints multiple copies of the page.

Selecting a Service Bureau

When seeking an imaging service, you need to find out what equipment they offer. Is their imagesetter a capstan unit or drum unit? What kinds of scanners do they have? What kind of removable mass storage devices?

Many users of Microsoft Windows have found that some service bureaus have trouble with files created with programs that run in this environment. For all the strides that Windows has made, most service bureaus are still geared toward Macintosh output. Find out how experienced they are in working with Windows.

Also ask about their service. What kind of turnaround time do they guarantee? Many service bureaus have different rates depending on how quickly you need the job. You can pay as much as double the normal amount if you need the job immediately.

Finally, make a subjective judgment. Are these people you think you can work with? Will they work with you to ensure that you get the best possible output of your job? Are they knowledgeable about the technical issues involved in image capture and output?

As noted before, service bureaus can be valuable allies in your quest to get good-looking images—but sometimes they can also seem like your worst enemy.

Going to Print

In most cases, the final stop on your imaging journey is the quick printer or commercial lithographer. Quick printers, such as PIP and Sir Speedy, are characterized by storefront operations, and typically handle black-and-white or spot color jobs in print volumes of 5000 or less. Commercial printers generally operate from large plants and offer more sophisticated equipment, such as four-color presses and binding equipment.

Many commercial printers have specialties, such as books, magazines, newspapers, direct mail, annual reports, or packaging. Because they are set up to provide this specialty, they may be able to offer more cost-effective or higher-quality service.

Most commercial printers use what are known as "sheetfed" presses, which print on cut sheets of paper. The presses are typically defined by the maximum size of the sheet they can handle and the number of colors they can print in a single run. For example, a four-color press has a quartet of units in which plates can be mounted. Such presses can thus print all four CMYK process colors in a single run.

Most commercial printers use sheetfed presses, as shown here in the background.

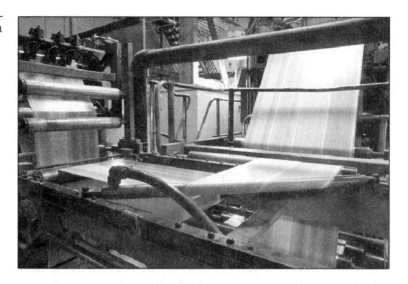

A web press prints on a roll of paper.

Although the press prints on individual sheets, the sheets are almost always cut in some manner after they come off the press. In many cases, the printer will go "multiple up," producing two or more pages on a single sheet, which is then cut in the binding and finishing department.

A "web" press, typically used for high-volume jobs like newspapers, magazines, and books, prints on large rolls of paper. In most cases, a web press prints on forms known as signatures, which are folded and cut when the job comes off the press. Web presses fall into two categories that determine the kind of paper they can print on. A "heat-set" or "UV-set" web press can print on coated (glossy) paper. The name comes from the need to apply heat (or ultraviolet light) to the job as it is printed. If the web press is not heat-set, it is limited to printing on uncoated stocks.

Many commercial printers have installed electronic prepress departments with imagesetters and other digital equipment. They are sort of like service bureaus and print shops in a single location. The advantage of this arrangement is that the prepress department knows exactly what kind of output the press department needs to get the best possible print quality. You also get the convenience of one-stop shopping.

New Printing Technologies

During the past several years, the printing industry has undergone a major upheaval caused by electronic prepress technology. Now the industry faces an even bigger revolution as digital technology moves into the arena of the press itself. Several new technologies have emerged that allow printers to offer services or quality levels they could not provide before. These include digital presses, HiFi Color, and waterless printing.

All of these technologies have implications for the use of scanned images. Because they are so new, print buyers and printers alike are still developing the expertise needed to take full advantage of the new capabilities.

Digital Presses

One recent trend in the commercial printing market is the digital press. This is a printing press that can accept output directly from computer files, bypassing the need to

The Indigo E-Print 1000 is a digital color press.

create film from an imagesetter. Some use a variation of offset printing technology, while others are toner-based products that offer print speeds comparable to offset.

These presses are likely to usher in a new era of what's known as "on-demand" printing. In traditional lithography, high set-up expenses—including the creation of film and plates—make it impractical to print color pieces in small quantities. In digital printing, there are no film separations, no plates, and none of the other prepress steps that add to the cost of a print job. As a result, you can produce just as many copies as you need, when you need them.

In many ways, the digital printing process has more in common with going to a PostScript device than working a conventional press. This is one reason why many such products are finding homes in digital prepress facilities rather than print shops.

The first digital press to be introduced, Heidelberg's GTO-DI, is really a conventional sheetfed press retrofitted with computer-to-plate technology. Plates are mounted on the press, just as on a traditional press, except in this case they are blank. Laser printheads in the press—one for each process color—image the plate from digital data as it is mounted. The GTO-DI's use of conventional offset technology is both a plus and a minus: a plus because it offers sheetfed quality and works with standard inks and supplies, a minus because it requires at least some of the set-up of a conventional press. It is best suited for press runs ranging from about 1000 to 10,000.

Other digital presses, such as the Indigo E-Print and Xeikon DCP-1, are best suited for press runs ranging from 50 to 500. These are true digital presses in that they produce output directly from computer files without the need to create a plate.

The E-Print was the first truly digital offset press. The device, which looks more like a copier than a printing press, uses a rotating drum that can be re-imaged with each turn. The same drum thus applies each of the CYMK inks to the page. Among other advantages, the technology allows for personalization of each page printed. As a result, you could conceivably create a newspaper with each recipient's name in a headline. Indigo offers another press, the Omnius, that can apply images directly to packaging materials.

The DCP-1 and Chromapress both use a toner-based printing engine developed by Xeikon. The DCP-1 is designed to run with a variety of front-end computers, while the Chromapress uses an Agfa front-end. The press prints on roll-fed paper, adding flexibility to the kinds of formats that can be produced.

The Xeikon print engine uses a continuous-tone process, with the ability to produce 64 shades of each color. The early consensus among imaging users is that the Indigo E-Print offers somewhat better image quality, but the Xeikon is less expensive to operate, which should result in lower prices for printing.

This is a fast-moving technology, and we are likely to see new competitors in this market for some time to come.

HiFi Color

HiFi Color is a new technology that replaces traditional four-color process with six, seven, or eight process colors. The technology is being promoted by a printing industry consultant named Mills Davis, who established the HiFi Color Project in 1992. The project includes hardware and software vendors, press manufacturers, and commercial printers, about 100 companies in all.

The advantage of HiFi color is that it expands the gamut of colors that can be printed on an offset press. Pieces printed with HiFi color tend to have strong, vibrant colors that grab attention.

To produce HiFi color, your printer needs software that can convert CMYK images into one of the alternative processes. One of the first products in this category was Pantone's Hexachrome, which uses yellow, orange, magenta, blue, green, and black. Others include DuPont's HyperColor, Linotype-Hell's EderMCS, and Scitex's ResoLUT PS.

HiFi Color also requires sophisticated screening. In the last chapter, we noted that in CYMK color separations, dots in each of the process colors are printed at different angles to avoid conflict. When you add two or three additional process colors, you begin to run out of room in the rosette. This is why many experts believe HiFi color to be a good match for stochastic screening.

Waterless Printing

The traditional offset printing process uses a dampening system in which ink is mixed with water. But some printers use an offset printing technique that removes water from the process. Strangely enough, this process is known as "waterless printing." The technology permits reproduction of images with rich, vibrant colors and extremely high line screens, equivalent to as much as 600 lines per inch.

If you want to "go waterless," as they say, you—or more precisely your imaging service—needs an imagesetter capable of producing high-resolution screens.

Help from Your Commercial Printer

Your commercial printer can be a valuable resource in helping you get the best possible reproduction of your scanned images and your print job in general. Whether you produce film at a separate imaging service or allow your printer to handle the entire job, it is a good idea to discuss the project with the printer before you begin.

One area where your printer can help is in paper selection. The stock on which your job is printed has a major impact on how the pages look when they roll off the press. A job printed on newsprint or another uncoated stock will look much different from one printed on coated stock. For example, uncoated stocks—especially newsprint—tend to create a high level of dot gain, in which ink spreads slightly when it is laid on the page. The result is that the image looks darker than it should because the dots are larger. You can compensate for this in Photoshop or another image-editing program by using a transfer curve to lighten the image. But it is also possible that your printer or prepress facility automatically adjusts output to account for dot gain as well. Only by communicating with your imaging service ahead of time will you learn exactly what you need to do to make your printed communications look their best.

If you plan to use one of the newer printing technologies, such as a digital press or HiFi color, then it is even more important to communicate with your printer. The scanning parameters that work with a conventionally printed job may not be effective with a digital or waterless press. Your printer is in the best position to steer you through the maze of new technologies that are making our work easier and more complicated at the same time.

CHAPTER 9

Document Imaging

For most of this book, we have discussed the benefits of using scanners for the input and manipulation of images. But through a process known as Optical Character Recognition (OCR), scanners can be taught to read words as well. With the addition of a software package, a scanner can be used to convert characters on paper into a text file on disk that you can edit with your word processor. Think of it as hiring a fast, inexpensive typist.

In this chapter, we'll look at how OCR software can be used to improve productivity in a wide range of situations. We'll also discuss document scanners that allow organizations to convert large volumes of documents—including text and graphics—into digital files that can be easily be searched and retrieved from a database. And, since this is the last chapter in the book, we'll conclude the chapter by making some general observations about the future of scanning.

Optical Character Recognition

Some might look at OCR as a way of bridging the old—information on paper—and the new—information in digital form on a computer screen. If they remain in good condition, reports, records, articles, and other paper documents created years ago can be entered into today's computer systems with relative ease, allowing their use with word processors, database management programs, and other software packages. If you work with people who still rely on those quaint contraptions known as typewriters, you can use their output with your computer.

At the same time, despite the hopeful predictions of office automation experts, computers have not created the "paperless office." Instead, information in hard copy form (as it is known) seems to pile up in greater amounts than ever. After all, those millions of laser printers that fueled the desktop publishing revolution aren't churning out chocolate cupcakes. How many of those laser-printed pages that cross your desk would you want to store on disk?

The first scanners released on the market 20 years ago—bulky monsters that cost tens of thousands of dollars—were OCR devices used for rapid input of text. Many were used in the newspaper business, allowing reporters to write their articles on typewriters, the pages from which were then scanned into the OCR system. Today, you can spend less than $1000 for a scanner/OCR software combo that is much more powerful than those bulky systems of old.

OCR Applications

OCR capability is helpful in any situation where text on paper must be used in a computer. The most common function that comes to mind is straight text entry: using your scanner and OCR software as a quiet, fast typist. If you already own a scanner or plan to purchase one, chances are good that you do some sort of desktop publishing. In most cases, you probably use text that's submitted by disk or electronic mail, but in many cases, you might get an article printed on a laser printer or otherwise unavailable in digital form. Or perhaps you publish press releases with little or no rewriting. In all of these cases, OCR software can save you the hassle of typing the text in manually.

Data Entry

Another use of OCR is as a data entry tool for database management programs or spreadsheets. If you keep paper

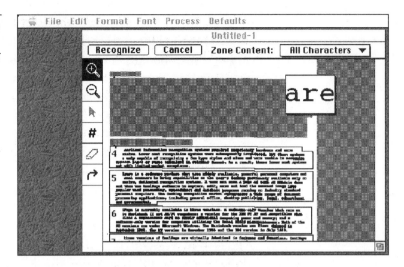

files where records are typed in a consistent format, for example, you may be able to scan the text into an ASCII file, which can then be converted to a database format with relatively little effort. Information from printed financial reports can be read into a worksheet. In some cases, you may need special software in addition to your OCR package to translate data into the proper format.

OCR can even provide a means of translating data between incompatible computer systems. The sly geniuses who make fortunes thinking up new computer products have given us many ways to convert data among various hardware and software formats. But if you have an old CP/M or Apple II computer with no easy means of moving the data to a Mac or PC, you can print the files out and scan them into your new system.

Building a Database

OCR products that can scan typeset pages from a magazine or book present the possibility of building large databases of published information. Magazine and newspaper editors could scan back issues of their publications, building electronic archives of past articles. Students and researchers could scan material from encyclopedias, journals, and other references for use in a retrievable database.

The ability to store published articles by means of OCR raises obvious legal questions. Most material published in magazines, books, and newspapers is copyrighted. To reproduce it in most situations, you are legally required to obtain the publisher's permission. The same law, however, applies to photocopies of copyrighted articles, and how many people honor those copyrights? It is unlikely that someone who builds a files of scanned articles for personal use will suffer legal consequences. But anyone who builds such a database for commercial purposes could be in for trouble.

OCR Features

All OCR packages have the same basic function: to recognize text and convert it to a computer-readable form. But beyond this, features and capabilities can vary widely. Early programs required that you spend a considerable amount of time training them to recognize specific fonts. Most packages available today offer "omnifont" capability, meaning they can recognize text without prior instruction from the user. Some offer extra features like spell-checkers that are designed especially for spotting common OCR mistakes, such as the letter "b" being recognized as "lo." Others allow you to specify substitution characters when they see a symbol. For example, if the software sees a "TM," it translates the symbol into the word "trademark."

Some OCR packages have special features that allow them to recognize text from faxes or dot-matrix printers. Because the characters tend to be broken, this kind of output causes fits for many OCR packages. Some packages compensate for the broken output by filling in the gaps, allowing them to recognize the characters. Another nice feature in some OCR programs is the ability to screen out color backgrounds or reversed text.

Hardware

Hardware requirements for most OCR applications are pretty simple. You don't need a flatbed scanner or gray-scale capability, but you do need a scanner with at least

300-dpi resolution. Higher resolution is helpful if you want to scan small typefaces. An automatic sheet feeder can also be handy if you intend to scan a lot of pages, but be sure the OCR software supports document feeding.

Some OCR packages, particularly the more sophisticated page recognition programs, require a large amount of memory to process image data. If you have to scan a page and save it with your scanner control software before performing character recognition, you'll need enough memory to hold a full-page TIFF or PCX file.

Several companies sell OCR software designed for use with hand-held scanners. A user runs the device line by line across the page, watching characters appear in succession on the screen. The scanning hardware is less expensive than sheetfed or flatbed scanners, but dependence on the operator to control the scanning process makes hand-held devices somewhat cumbersome, especially with many pages of text. They can be useful, however, if you only need to scan selected portions of reports or records.

OCR packages can use scanner output in one of two ways. The preferred way is for the program to control the scanner directly. All scanning parameters and commands are set from within the OCR software. When you give the Scan command, an image of the page is read directly into the program. A vendor-supplied package should be able to do this with little problem, but many third-party packages can also control popular scanners.

Many OCR programs allow you to specify multiple regions on the page that will be recognized.

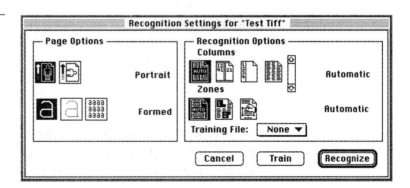

Scan Transparencies in a Pinch

APPLICATION BRIEF

Even if you do not have a transparency scanner or transparency option for your flatbed scanner, you can sometimes get away with capturing low-quality or for-position-only quality from your transparency on a flatbed. One method is to place a light table on top of the transparency on the glass of the scanner. The illumination coming from above may be enough to pick up details in the film. Or you can try moving a small flourescent desk lamp over the scanner glass as the scanning head moves down the surface of the platen. This technique requires a steady hand, however.

An OCR package can also use scanner output by reading image files in standard graphics formats. Using your scanner control program, you scan a printed page and save it as a TIFF or PCX file. Then you exit the scanner program, run the OCR software, and read in the image file. The software recognizes the type in the image file as if it were a printed page. This approach is obviously less convenient than direct scanning, but it does allow the OCR packages to work with many kinds of scanned output.

Accuracy

The most important feature of OCR software, of course, is its accuracy. To be at all useful, an OCR package should have an accuracy rating of 99 percent or more. This may sound high, but remember that one mistake out of a hundred translates into more than one for every two lines.

Many OCR programs use special techniques to improve the speed and accuracy of the character recognition process. Some, for example, feature a spreadsheet mode that is especially "tuned" to recognize numbers. Some will prompt you when an unrecognized character is encountered, allowing you to enter it into the pattern-matching library.

Some have built-in dictionaries that allow them to place characters in context, enhancing accuracy. For example, if the OCR software recognizes the word "recogni?e," it would know to substitute a "z" for the question mark.

One difference among packages is what they do when they don't recognize a character. Some will make the best guess they can, adding characters that amount to gibberish. Others insert specially designated characters, usually determined by the user, in place of unrecognizable letters. Later, you can use a search and replace feature in your word processor to find the special character and enter the correct spelling.

File Formats

Most OCR packages produce text in the ASCII file format. ASCII is a text file format that can be understood by almost any database, spreadsheet, or word processing program. But not all programs that read or write ASCII can necessarily use an ASCII file produced by another program as-is. In ASCII text files, for example, each line is followed by a carriage return. Most word-processing programs, on the other hand, place a carriage return only after each paragraph. A program may be able to read ASCII files, but you have to manually remove unwanted carriage returns or use some sort of utility software to do it for you. For a spreadsheet program to read ASCII, the file must be in a worksheet format, with consistent rows and columns.

To make the user's life easier, some OCR packages can produce files directly in popular word processing formats, such as WordPerfect or Microsoft Word. With some, you can retain formatting codes for boldface and other effects. Another nice feature is the ability to convert tables and other documents directly into spreadsheet files.

Training

One key difference among OCR packages is whether they require training. It used to be that most packages had to "learn" how a particular font looked in order to recognize it. After scanning a page containing the font, the program isolated each character, displaying it on the screen for the user to identify. If you saw a character that looked like an "E," for example, you typed in an "E" from the keyboard. The software then knew that the character shape was an "E." As you went through the page, character by character, the program built a library of recognized letters, numbers, and symbols known as a type table. Once the software was trained, you could scan other pages containing the font with reasonable assurance that the software will recognize them accurately.

The problem with trainable packages was that they sometimes took so long to train you were better off just typing in the text manually. Most packages these days offer "omnifont" capability in which they can recognize nearly any typeface without training. These programs use a sophisticated technique known as topological analysis or feature extraction. The software analyzes the shape of each character, using a method similar to the brain's own cognitive processes. If a line descends on a slope to a baseline and then ascends again at a 45-degree angle, the software recognizes it as a V.

Some omnifont OCR programs incorporate training as an option. This is useful for scanning documents with unusual typefaces or symbols. In some cases, you can train the software to insert a complete word in the text when it encounters a certain symbol. For example, it will write out the word "trademark" when it encounters the symbol ™.

Tips for Using OCR

In general, remember that the cleaner the original copy—and your scanner's platen—the more accurate the OCR translation will be. Smudges, white-out, and other markings, even subtle ones, can introduce distortions and reduce accuracy. Adjusting the brightness control on your scanner can improve the readability of certain documents. Sometimes you may be better off using a photocopy of a page if the copy can be made with sharper contrast than the original. You might even try using a graphics program to clean up a scanned page before turning your OCR software loose on it.

A good spelling checker will be worth its weight in gold if you plan to scan a lot of text. Even if the OCR package has special character substitution, it will no doubt make some mistakes in characters it thinks it recognizes. A spelling checker can quickly identify words that don't make sense. You should still remember, however, to proofread carefully any text scanned in with an OCR package. No spelling checker in the world is going to flag the word "pet" when it's really supposed to be "pot." But it can cut down dramatically on proofreading time. And

Scan Forms for On-Screen Data Entry

APPLICATION BRIEF
Most people spend a good deal of time filling out forms for business, personal, and tax purposes. A desktop scanner can be a handy companion for filling out forms without having to resort to a typewriter or handwriting. Place the form on the scanner as straight as possible and scan it to a line-art (one-bit-per-pixel) format. Be sure to scan the entire 8 1/2 by 11 inch page. Bring the scanned image into your publishing program at 100 percent size, aligning the upper-left corner of the image to the upper-left corner of your on-screen page. To make it easier to enter text on the form, you may want to place the image of the form on a master page or on a layer that can be viewed but not moved. This will make it easier to enter text. When you're done entering the text, print the page to your laser printer. As an alternative, you can print just the text only, using the "omit pictures" option of your publishing program. Then feed the form through your laser printer's manual feed slot, and—if you've lined things up properly—you should get the text to print in just the right places on the form.

when you do proofread, do it on paper. It can be difficult to catch typos on a computer screen.

File Conversion

File conversions present special challenges for users of OCR packages. Fortunately, the ASCII text files created by most OCR packages can be used by most other software packages, though minor modifications may be needed. As we noted above, to use an ASCII file in a program like WordPerfect, you must strip carriage returns from each line, except at the end of each paragraph. In most cases, this kind of operation can be performed with your word processor's search-and-replace function.

If you plan to use OCR as a data entry tool for spreadsheets or databases, your task may be more difficult. You can make it easier if you can define the format in which the pages are typed. If entering records to a database, for example, it would be quite easy to use OCR if a typewritten page contained the data in what's known as delimited ASCII format. That is, each record occupies one line of the file, and each piece of information in the records is separated with a comma and quotation marks.

In most cases, however, you won't have the luxury of determining the format of typewritten pages to be scanned in. A list of names and addresses may be printed in address label format, but it won't do you much good if you need it in the delimited ASCII format that your database program can understand. If your word processor has a strong search-and-replace function, you can use it to convert a mailing list to delimited ASCII.

Document Scanners

Throughout most of this book, we have talked about scanners that produce images for use in publishing and graphics applications. There is another class of scanner, however, that captures complete pages for later retrieval on screen. In many ways, these document scanners are a replacement of microfiche and microfilm systems that many libraries, corporations, and government agencies have used for years.

The advantages of a digital document retrieval system are obvious. There is much more flexibility in retrieving, displaying, and printing documents once they have been stored in this manner. The digital images can be used in other electronic publishing applications. And with the help of document retrieval software, you can perform some powerful search and cataloging functions that you could never do with an analog document retrieval system.

The scanners used in document retrieval systems are typically faster and more flexible than scanners used for image capture. They generally incorporate a sheet feeder for for multi-page documents. And they generally cost more too.

Once a document is scanned and stored, it can be retrieved using software packages like PageKeeper, Dragnet, PaperMaster, and Acrobat Catalog. These programs allow you to enter keywords, then search through the database of documents to locate those that include the words you've entered.

Document scanners, such as the Kodak Imagelink 923, are designed for capturing long documents such as reports, proposals, and articles.

Portable Documents

In addition to document retrieval software, several companies offer products that make it easy to exchange documents among different computer systems. If a document contains nothing but ASCII text, moving it from one system to another is a simple operation, but such is not the case if it includes graphics and formatted text in different typefaces. For example, you have no way of knowing if the fonts in your system will be present on other systems on which the documents will be viewed, or if those systems have software capable of displaying the images in the file.

Programs like Adobe Acrobat and Common Ground offer a way to exchange graphical documents not just among different computers, but among different operating systems.

Acrobat uses technology based on Adobe's PostScript page description language. Instead of printing your document to a PostScript printer, you "print" it to a special file format called PDF. Once a document has been converted to the PDF format, it can be viewed by any computer user who has a piece of software known as an Acrobat Reader. Readers are available for Windows, Macintosh, DOS, and Unix computers. The readers are free, and can be distributed along with the PDF files you want your friends or associates to read (Adobe makes its money selling the software used to create PDF files). In addition to viewing the files, users can also search and retrieve text or print the document on a laser printer.

The Future of Scanning

One challenge in writing a book about a fast-moving technology such as scanners is dealing with future trends. Hardware and software vendors introduce new products on what seems like a daily basis. You can be sure that whatever piece of hardware or software we've described here, someone will try to introduce a competing product

Adobe Acrobat offers users an electronic document medium for displaying scanned images.

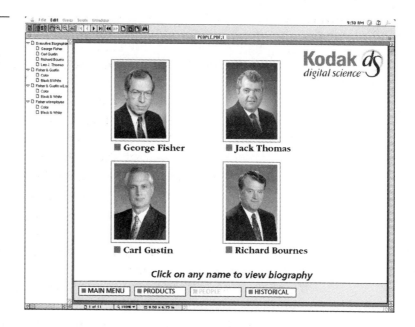

that performs the same task more efficiently and at lower cost. Then, of course, the first vendor will prepare an upgrade that drops the upstart competitor to second place, and the cycle begins anew.

Then there are the truly groundbreaking products that perform some important function in a completely new way. One recent example is HSC's Live Picture software, which uses a new model for editing and compositing images.

If the market moves so fast, you might wonder why we bother to write such a book at all. But even though the products change, the basic needs of scanning users remain the same, as do the fundamental processes by which we capture images and produce them in print. So all is not lost, and we have every reason to believe that the information in this book will remain useful for years (or at least months) to come.

One thing we can be sure of is that the desktop computers we use in five or ten years will be much more powerful than the ones we use now. In 1982, a desktop computer was considered a powerhouse if it had 64 kilobytes of RAM and could store 360 kilobytes of data on its disks. Today, it is not uncommon to find computers with 64 megabytes of RAM and 1.2 gigabytes of disk storage.

Software applications, taking advantage of these added hardware capabilities, will offer more features and, through artificial intelligence and fuzzy logic, will sometimes seem to think for themselves. All of these developments will have impact on imaging applications.

We have seen that the input, storage, and manipulation of scanned images requires substantial hardware resources, resources that will no doubt grow in abundance as time marches on. Graphic images, particularly color images, consume vast amounts of data. Storage capacities keep growing as the cost-per-megabyte falls, and this trend is likely to continue.

Given more memory and processing speed, along with the decision-making capabilities promised by artificial intelligence, imaging software will offer features that make current programs pale by comparison. A package, for example, might be able to take a scanned page containing text and graphics, separate the two, then perform image enhancements on the graphic area and optical character recognition on the text. The software would translate the text into a foreign language and use it to replace the original copy on the page, printing out the altered document. And the software would automatically perform such image-enhancement functions as equalization.

Another trend in the microcomputer industry is the growing importance of communications and networking. This is especially so in the publishing arena, where the division of labor requires the ability to exchange text and graphics files among writers, editors, and designers. Within a local-area network, images can be scanned at one workstation, touched up at a second, and incorporated into a desktop publishing system at a third. Wide-area networks permit similar connectivity among computer users in separate facilities, whether next door or across an ocean. You could scan an image in Los Angeles, for example, and have it incorporated into a magazine page layout in New York. Again, these capabilities are made possible by more-powerful microcomputers that can handle the complex task of managing multiple users in an interconnected system.

We've all heard about the Information Superhighway, the much publicized digital network that will revolutionize our society in much the same way television changed everyone's lives in the 1950s and 60s. In the future, they say, all communications—telephone, television, and media that don't yet exist—will flow into our homes and offices as bits and bytes.

All of this has interesting implications for the use of desktop scanners. On one hand, if all information is handled in digital form, it would seem that scanners will soon become obsolete. What point is there in scanning a photograph or document if it is already available in a digital format? Why scan a photograph into your system if you can simple capture the image with a digital camera?

On the other hand, plenty of information remains on paper, and as our society moves even more into the digital realm, there will be tremendous demand for converting this information into computer images.

Despite the talk of the Information Superhighway, paper remains an excellent medium for the presentation of information—at least until they invent a computer that matches the resolution of ink on paper, one that you can fold and place in your shirt pocket if you so desire. So paper will be with us for a long time, and as long as images and text remain on paper, there will be a need for products that convert that information into the zeroes and ones that computers handle so well.

Glossary of Terms

Analog. A method of representing information by direct transfer of the changing elements. A clock with hour and minute hands shows analog information, while a clock with an LCD display shows digital information.

Architecture. The specific components, and the way those components are interconnected, that make up a microcomputer system. Often used to describe the specific bus structure within a microcomputer.

ASCII. American Standard Code for Information Interchange. A standard coding system that assigns a numeric value to letters, numbers and symbols. The lowest common denominator for exchanging text among programs.

Aspect Ratio. The relationship between the height and width of a displayed object. A 1:1 aspect ratio means the object will appear undistorted.

Auto Trace. A feature found in some graphics programs that allows conversion of bit-mapped images into an object-oriented format. See Bit-map, Object-oriented graphics.

Bernoulli. A removable hard disk system popular in the PC-compatible. Bernoulli disks can hold 44 or 90 megabytes of data and are manufactured by Iomega Corp.

Bezier Curves. A type of curve created by some object-oriented graphics programs that can be manipulated by means of endpoints and anchor points that determine its slope and length.

Binary. A numbering system employed by most computer systems that uses two numerals, 0 and 1, to represent all numbers.

Bit-Map. Images formed by patterns of dots, as opposed to object-oriented images, where shapes are formed from mathematical descriptions.

Bit-Mapped Display. A computer display that can control individual pixels, allowing the computer to show graphics in addition to text. See Character-Based Display.

Bit. The smallest unit of binary information. A bit will have a value of "1" or "0". A contracted acronym derived from Binary digIT.

Brightness. A measure of lightness or darkness in an image.

Bus. A data pathway within a computer system.

Byte. A unit of data containing eight bits. A byte can consist of up to 256 different values. Used as a measure of file size on a computer. See Kilobyte, Megabyte.

Calibration. A process by which a scanner, monitor, or output device is adjusted to provide more accurate display and reproduction of images.

Camera-Ready Copy. Text and illustrations laid out on a page in the proper size and position, and ready to be photographed for a printing plate. See Mechanicals.

Cathode-Ray Tube. (CRT). A vacuum tube that generates and guides electrons onto a fluorescent screen to produce images, characters, or graphics.

CCD. See Charge-Coupled Device.

CD-ROM. (Compact-Disc Read-Only Memory) An optical disc capable of storing computer data. Often used for distribution of clip art, fonts, and multimedia titles. Data can be read from a CD-ROM, but cannot be written to the disc.

Central Processing Unit (CPU). The main section of a computer, which handles arithmetic and logic operations.

CGM. see Computer Graphics Metafile.

Character-Based Display. A computer display, commonly found in the first personal computers, that is limited to showing alphanumeric characters and simple graphic elements. Most character-based displays use a grid consisting of 25 rows and 80 columns. Each cell in the grid can contain only a single character.

Charge-Coupled Device (CCD). An image sensor used in scanners and digital cameras.

Clipboard. A temporary electronic storage area in a computer system where text or graphics can be held for reuse.

Color Correction. A process of adjusting color values to achieve the best level of accuracy for a reproduction.

Color Separation. A process by which a color page is converted into CYMK color components. Each color can be used to create a piece of film, which is burned onto a plate or written directly to a printing press. See CYMK.

Color Separations. A set of four transparencies for making plates in four-color printing.

Comp. See Comprehensive.

Compact Disc Read-Only Memory (CD-ROM). An optical disc that conforms to a standard industry format in which information can be read from the medium, but not written to it. A CD-ROM can store between 600 and 700 megabytes.

Comprehensive. A page, produced during the design process, that provides a preview of how the final print job will look.

Computer Graphics Metafile (CGM). A file format used for storing computer graphics.

Continuous Tone. A photograph or illustration containing an infinite range of colors or gray shades.

Contrast. A measure of the difference among various colors or gray levels in an image. A high-contrast image shows a large difference between light and dark shades. A low-contrast image shows less difference between light and dark shades.

CPU. See Central Processing Unit.

Crop Marks. Small marks on a page that indicate the area to be printed.

Crop. To cut or trim an illustration or other graphic element.

CRT. See Cathode-Ray Tube.

CYMK. Cyan, Yellow, Magenta, Black. These four colors are used by printers to reproduce color images.

Data Compression. An operation that reduces the memory space required to store image data.

Default. A specification that takes effect in the absence of other instructions. Most scanner programs have default settings for variables like brightness and contrast that apply unless the user requests something else.

Densitometer. A device used to measure the intensity of gray shades or colors in a printed image. Often used to calibrate an imagesetter, scanner, or monitor for more accurate display and reproduction of images.

Desktop Publishing. The use of a personal computer to produce camera-ready page layouts for books, newsletters, magazines, and other printed material. Also refers to programs that produce page layouts. See Page-Layout Program.

Dialog Box. A pop-up window in a program that allows the user to choose among different options.

Diffusion. A filtering effect performed on gray-scale or color images that randomly distributes gray levels in small areas of an image to achieve a mezzotint effect.

Digital. A general description for information stored in the form of zeroes and ones (bits and bytes) in a computer system.

Digital Halftone. A halftone produced by a computer system. See Halftone.

Digitize. To convert information to the digital format usable by a computer. What scanners and digitizers do.

Digitizer. A device that converts video signals into a digital format that can be displayed on a computer. Also used to refer to certain computer drawing devices.

Disk Operating System (DOS). An operating system for IBM-compatible personal computers that controls basic computer operations, such as the transfer of data to and from a disk drive. Requires use of English-like commands to perform operations. Also known as MS-DOS and PC-DOS.

Dithering. A process by which an input or output device simulates shades of gray in an image by grouping dots into clusters known as halftone cells. See Halftone cell.

DOS. See Disk Operating System.

Dot. The smallest unit that can be printed, scanned, or displayed on a monitor. Dots produced on a laser printer are sometimes called spots.

Dots Per Inch (DPI). A unit that describes the resolution of an output device or monitor.

DPI. See Dots Per Inch.

Driver. A software program that controls a specific hardware device such as a frame grabber board, scanner, or printer.

Drum Imagesetter. An imagesetter in which the output media is mounted on a rotating drum.

Drum Scanner. A scanner in which reflective or transmissive media are mounted on a rotating drum.

Duotone. An image in which a single extra color is added to a black-and-white halftone.

Dye Sublimation. A color printing technology used in continuous-tone printers.

Edge Enhancement. An operation that accentuates the edge details of an image.

Electrostatic Plotter. An output device that uses a color xerographic process to produce large-format output.

Encapsulated PostScript (EPS). A file format that stores images in the form of PostScript language commands.

EPS. See Encapsulated PostScript File.

Equalization. A process by which the range of gray or color shades in an image is expanded to make the image more attractive.

Facsimile. A technology that allows transmission of images over telephone lines by use of facsimile machines or PC fax boards.

Filter. A software function that modifies an image by altering the gray or color values of certain pixels.

Flatbed scanner. A scanner, resembling a small photocopier, in which the image to be scanned is placed on a glass platen.

Font. All letters, numbers, and symbols in one size and typeface. Helvetica Bold Italic is a typeface. 12-point Helvetica bold italic is a font. Font is sometimes used interchangeably with typeface.

Four-color printing. A process that allows a printing press to reproduce most colors by mixing the three primary colors (cyan, yellow, magenta) and black.

Frame Buffer. Memory used to store an array of graphic or pictorial image data. Each element of the array corresponds to one or more pixels in a video display or one or more dots on a laser printer or other output device.

Frame-Grabber Board. An image processing board that samples, digitizes, stores and processes video signals. Typically, a frame grabber board will plug into one expansion slot within a microcomputer.

Frame. A block positioned on a page into which the user can place text or graphics.

Front-end. A computer workstation that sends data to an output device, such as an inkjet or electrostatic plotter.

Galley. In typesetting terminology, a reproduction of a column of type, usually printed on a long paper sheet.

Gamma Correction. A process by which the user adjusts the midtone contrast and brightness of an image.

Gamma Curve Editor. A function found in many imaging programs that allows the user to perform gamma correction operations on a color or gray-scale image. Also known as a Gray or Color Map Editor.

Graphical User Interface (GUI). A computer interface, such as Microsoft Windows, characterized by the use of a bit-mapped display and graphical icons that represent common computer functions.

Gray Component Replacement (GCR). A prepress operation that improves the quality of color reproduction by changing the balance of inking. The amount of ink used to print yellow, magenta, and cyan is decreased, while black is increased to produce a stronger image. Similar to undercolor removal (UCR).

Gray Scale Value. A number with a range between 0 and 255 that represents the brightness level of an individual pixel in a gray scale image document.

Gray Scale. A measure of the number of gray levels in an image. Also used to describe the ability to display multiple levels of gray.

GUI. See Graphical User Interface.

Halftone cell. A halftone dot created on a laser printer or imagesetter. The cell is created by grouping printer dots into a grid. The more dots present in the grid, the larger the cell appears.

Halftone. A type of photograph that can be reproduced by a printing press. A halftone breaks a continuous-tone photo into tiny dots, which the press can reconstruct with ink. The eye interprets the dots as tones and shades. The density of the dot pattern, called a screen, determines the ultimate quality of the printed reproduction. A halftone can be a positive or a negative. See Screen.

Hand Scanner. A small scanner that requires the user to manually move the unit over the image to be scanned.

Hardware. Mechanical, magnetic, electronic, and electrical devices that make up computer. Physical equipment that makes up a computer system.

Hercules. A monochrome graphics display standard used in the PC-compatible environment. See CGA, EGA, VGA.

Histogram. A graph showing the distribution of gray or color levels within an image. The horizontal coordinate is the pixel value. The vertical coordinate shows the number of pixels in the image that use the value. Histograms give a good indication of image contrast and brightness dynamic range.

Horizontal Resolution. The number of pixels contained in a single horizontal scanning line.

Illustration Program. A program used to create object-oriented graphics. See Object-Oriented Graphics.

Imagesetter. A high-resolution output device, descended from the phototypesetter, that produces output on film or photographic paper at resolutions of 1000 dots per inch or more. Usually employs a page description language like PostScript.

Inkjet Printer. A nonimpact printer that uses droplets of ink. As a printhead moves across surface of paper, it shoots a stream of tiny, electrostatically-charged ink drops at the page, placing them to form characters.

Interpolation. A mathematical technique used in some scanning and graphics programs that can be used to increase the apparent resolution of an image. Computers usually store images as numbers that represent the intensity of the image at discrete points. Interpolation generates values for points in between these discrete points by looking at the surrounding intensities.

Joint Photographic Experts Group (JPEG). An international standard for compression and decompression of photographic images.

JPEG. See Joint Photographic Experts Group.

Kilobyte. A measurement unit used to describe the size of computer files. A kilobyte is equivalent to 1024 bytes or characters of information.

Landscape. Horizontal orientation of pages or screen displays. See Portrait.

Laser Printer. A non-impact output device that fuses toner to paper to create near-typeset quality text and graphics. The basic technology is similar to that of a photocopier.

Layout. The arrangement of a page, especially the spacing and position of text and graphics. Often used to describe a rough sketch.

LCD. See Liquid-Crystal Display.

LED. See Light-Emitting Diode.

Light-Emitting Diode (LED). A form of display lighting employed on many different office, reprographic, and consumer products.

Line Art. A drawing that contains no grays or middle tones. Even when cross-hatching and other techniques are used to simulate shading, line art is made up exclusively of black (lines) and white (paper).

Line Screen. A measure of the screen frequency, or resolution, of a halftone. Most printed halftones have line screens ranging from 65 lines per inch to 150 lines per inch.

Linotronic. The brand name for imagesetters manufactured by Linotype-Hell, including the Linotronic 330 and Linotronic 630.

Lithography. See Offset printing.

Local-Area Network (LAN). A system that connects microcomputers to one another, allowing them to share data and output devices.

Lossless. An image-compression function in which image data is not lost every time the compression is performed.

Lossy. An image-compression function in which image data is lost every time the compression is performed.

LPI. Abbreviation for lines per inch. Used to measure halftone resolution.

MacPaint. A graphic file format developed by Apple Computer that can store bit-mapped images at 72 dots per inch.

Mechanicals. Camera-ready pages on artboards or flats, with text and art in position. See Camera-ready copy.

Megabyte. A measurement unit used to describe the size of computer files. A megabyte is equivalent to 1024 kilobytes, or 1,048,576 characters of information.

Microprocessor. A single chip or integrated circuit containing an entire central processing unit for a personal computer or computer-based device.

Microsoft Windows. A graphical user interface developed by Microsoft Corp. for PC-compatible computers.

Modem. A device that allows computers to send and receive information over phone lines.

Moiré Pattern. An undesirable grid-like pattern in a digital halftone resulting from the superimposition of dot-screens at wrong screen angles. Usually occurs when a halftone has been rescanned or if a dithered image has been scaled.

Mouse. A small, hand-held device for positioning the cursor on the screen. When the mouse is rolled across the surface of the desk, the cursor moves a corresponding distance on the screen.

MS-DOS. A disk operating system used widely with personal computers and developed by Microsoft Corp.

MSP. The graphics format used by Microsoft Windows Paint.

Multimedia. A category of computer applications characterized by the combination of sound, video, and/or animation.

Object-Oriented Graphics. Graphic images created by means of mathematical descriptions. They can usually be displayed or printed at the full resolution of the monitor or output device, offering more precision than bit-mapped images.

OCR. See Optical Character Recognition.

Offset Printing. A widely used printing process in which a page is reproduced photographically on a metal plate attached to a revolving cylinder. Ink is transferred from the plate to a rubber blanket from which it is transferred to paper.

Operating System. Master programs that keep all of computer components working together, including application programs.

Optical Disk. A form of data storage in which a laser records data on a disk that can be read with a lower-power laser pickup. There are three types of optical disks: Read Only (RO), Write-Once Read Many (WORM), and two types of erasable: Thermo Magneto Optical (TMO) and Phase Change (PC).

Optical Character Recognition. A computer operation in which text on paper is scanned and converted to text files that can be edited with a word processor.

Page Description Language. A programming language, such as PostScript, that gives precise instructions for how a page should look to an output device. See PostScript.

Page Layout Program. A computer program that allows the user to create page layouts for newsletters, newspapers, magazines, and other printed materials. Also known as desktop publishing or page layout programs.

Paint Program. A program used to create bit-mapped graphics. See Bit-map.

Palette. The set of all colors available for screen displays.

Panning. Moving a graphic image inside a frame to see its various sections.

Pantone Matching System. A popular system for specifying spot colors. Each color has its own Pantone number by which it can be selected. See Spot color.

PC-compatible. A computer system compatible with the IBM-PC and its descendants.

PCX. A graphic file format developed by ZSoft. Supported by many scanners and publishing programs.

Photo CD. A technology developed by Eastman Kodak that allows storage of photographic images on a CD-ROM.

Pica. A printing measurement unit used to specify line lengths, margins, columns, gutters, and so on. Equivalent to 12 points, or about 1/6 of an inch.

PICT. A graphic file format developed by Apple Computer that can store bit-mapped or object-oriented images.

Pixel. A picture element, or the smallest addressable component of a displayable image. Used to describe resolution.

Plate. A thin, flexible sheet of metal, paper, or plastic used in offset printing. It contains a photographic reproduction of the page.

Point Size. The vertical measurement of type, equivalent to the distance between the highest ascender and lowest descender.

Point. A unit of measurement used in printing and typography that is roughly equivalent to 1/72 of an inch.

Portrait. Vertical orientation of a page or display. See Landscape.

Position stat. A photocopy or other reproduction of a halftone that is pasted onto a mechanical to show the printer how to crop and position the final image.

Posterization. A photographic effect in which the number of gray levels in an image is reduced to achieve a poster-like effect.

PostScript Clone. A page description language that emulates PostScript. In theory, a PostScript clone printer can produce any page that a true PostScript printer can produce.

PostScript. A page description language developed by Adobe Systems Inc. and used by many laser printers and phototypesetters. See Page description language.

Print Spooler. A program that temporarily stores a file to be printed until the output device is available.

Process Camera. A camera used in graphic arts to photograph mechanicals and create printing plates.

Process Colors. The four colors needed for four-color printing: yellow, magenta, cyan, and black. See Four-color printing.

Proof. A trial copy of a page or publication used to check accuracy. Also short for proofread, meaning to check for mistakes.

Protocol. A formal set of conventions governing format of data and control of information exchange between two communication devices.

RAM. See Random Access Memory.

Random Access Memory (RAM). Computer memory that can be read and changed. Data can be written to a particular location without having to sequence through previous locations. RAM is volatile, so all data is lost on power down.

Raster Graphics. Pictures sent to printer as bit maps (each element of picture is dot defined as black or white).

Raster-Image Processor (RIP). A piece of hardware that electronically prepares a page created on a computer system for output on an imagesetter or other device.

Read Only Memory (ROM). Computer memory containing fixed data that cannot be changed once programmed. Programming is accomplished during the manufacturing process.

Reduced Instruction Set Computer (RISC). A computer architecture that permits rapid processing speed.

Reflective Media. Print media, such as paper, that show images by reflecting light back to the eye.

Register Marks. Marks used to permit exact alignment of pages. Usually printed just outside the live area and then trimmed off. The standard register mark is a small circle with a cross inside.

Register. Precise alignment of printing plates or negatives.

Resolution. The density of dots or pixels on a page or display, usually measured in dots per inch. The higher the resolution, the smoother the appearance of text or graphics.

RGB. An abbreviation for Red, Green and Blue, the primary colors used in CRT display devices.

RISC. see Reduced Instruction Set Computer.

Scale. To change the size of a piece of artwork.

Scanner. A digitizing device that converts a piece of artwork into an electronic bit-map that can be loaded and manipulated by a software program. A means of converting hand-drawn art or photos into electronic form.

Screen Fonts. Digital typefaces used for screen display.

Screen. The pattern of dots used to make a halftone or tint. Halftone screens are measured in lines, equivalent to dots per inch. Tint screens are measured in percentages, with a 10-percent screen being very light and a 100-percent screen being totally black.

Separations. Transparencies or pages used for color reproduction. Each separation is used to reproduce a particular color. See Process color, four-color printing.

Sharpen. A filtering effect that enhances contrast around edges in an image.

Slide Scanner. An image scanner capable of scanning 35mm slides.

Small Computer Systems Interface (SCSI). An interface for connecting disks and other peripheral devices to computer systems. SCSI is defined by an American National Standards Institute (ANSI) standard and is widely used throughout the computer industry.

Soften. A filtering effect that decreases contrast in an image.

Solarization. A photographic effect achieved when a negative is briefly exposed to light. Some areas of the image are under-exposed, while others are over-exposed.

Spot Color. The use of one or more extra colors on a page, used to highlight specified page elements. Colors are usually specified as PMS codes. See Pantone Matching System.

Strip. To paste one piece of film, usually a halftone, into another piece of film containing a page. The film is then converted into a printing plate.

SyQuest. A removable hard disk system popular on the Macintosh. SyQuest disks can hold 44, 88, or 105 megabytes of data and are manufactured by several vendors.

Tagged Image File Format (TIFF). A graphics file format used to store color and gray-scale images.

Thermal Transfer. A technology used in many color printers in which ink or dye is transferred to the page using a heat process.

386. A computer system that uses the 80386 microprocessor from Intel.

Thumbnail. A rough layout of a page, usually used for planning purposes.

TIFF. See Tagged Image File Format.

Transmissive Media. Film-based media, such as 35 mm slides or transparencies, that require backlighting to be seen.

Transparency Scanner. An image scanner capable of scanning transparencies.

Typeface. A particular type design. See Font, Typeface Family.

Undercolor Removal (UCR). Increasing the quality of color reproduction by changing the balance of inking. The amount of ink used to print yellow, magenta, and cyan is decreased, while black is increased to produce a stronger image.

Unsharp Masking Enhancement. An operation that produces a sharpened version of an image.

VGA. Short for Video Graphics Array, a popular color display standard in the PC-compatible environment. See CGA, EGA, Hercules.

Virtual Memory. A hardware and software mechanism in which a hard disk is used as an extension of RAM.

Word Processor. A program used to enter, edit, and manipulate text.

Workstation. A full-featured desktop or deskside computer typically dedicated to a single person's use.

WYSIWYG. An acronym for What You See Is What You Get, meaning that text and graphics on a screen correspond closely to final printed output. Pronounced wizzy-wig.

Zoom. To view an enlarged (zoom in) or reduced (zoom out) portion of a page on screen.

GLOSSARY OF TERMS

INDEX

A

Add noise
    filter 96
Adobe Illustrator 78
Adobe Photoshop. *See* Photoshop
    gray map 107
Adobe Premiere 118
Analog
    informatio 24
ASCII
    defined 181
Aspect ratio
    defined 181
Auto-trace
    function of illustration software 117

B

Batch scanning 64
Bezier curve
    in illustration software 116
Bezier curves
    defined 181
Binary
    defined 181
Bitmap
    defined 182
Bits
    data in image 9
    defined 182
    depth of 26
BMP
    file format 79
Brightness
    control in image-editing software 99
    setting in software 67
Byte
    defined 182

C

Calibration
    defined 182
    of scanners 68
    options 70
    with gray map 100
CCDs
    as scanner's eyes 24
    defined 183
    in drum scanners 37
    resolution of 25
CD-ROM
    as multimedia form 119
    drives 55
    Photo CD discs 39
    putting scanned images on 22

Channels
    in color images 69
Charge-coupled device. *See* CCD
CIE 125
Clone
    tool 93
Clones
    PostScript 126
Color
    copiers 142
    correction 99
    HiFi 162
    management 16, 112
    management systems 74
    maps 100
    models 12–16
    perception 11–12
    primaries 13
    proofs 20
    reflective vs. transmissive 12
    scanners 28–30
    spaces 125
    spot vs. process 131
Color separations
    defined 183
    on imagesetter 130
    spot vs. process 131
ColorSync
    color management system 74
Commercial printers
    electronic prepress services 151
Compression
    of images 80
Comps
    producing on color printer 139
Continuous tone
    defined 183
    printers 123, 142
Contrast
    setting in software 67
Controllers
    PostScript 126
Copiers
    color 142
Copyright
    issues in scanned images 106
Corel Draw 117
Corel Ventura 112
Cromalins 138
Cropping
    as you scan 89
CYMK
    color model 14
    defined 183

D

Densitometer
    used in calibration 72
Device profiles
    in color management 74

Digital cameras
    as alternative to scanners   38
Digital Darkroom   88
Digital imaging   7
Digital printing   149, 160
Disk arrays   54
Displays   51
    24-bit   52
    perception of color on   11
Dithering
    as scanning option   63
    defined   184
    to simulate gray scale   27
Document feeder
    as flatbed option   34
Document scanners   174
Dodge and burn
    tools in image-editing software   94
Dot gain
    correcting   100
    in lithography   18
Dots
    defined   185
    halftone   127
    shape of   61, 132
Drum imagesetter
    defined   185
Drum scanners   30, 36
    desktop drum   37
Duotones
    defined   185
    separation of   131
Dye-sublimation printers   141
Dynamic range
    as scanner specification   29

E

Eastman Kodak. *See* Kodak. *See* Kodak
EFIcolor
    color management   112
Emboss
    filter in image-editing software   98
EPS
    file format   77
Equalization
    defined   185
Exapansion slots
    use of   48
Eyedropper
    tool in Photoshop   72

F

File formats
    for OCR   171
    Macintosh vs. PC   75
File size
    determining optimum   66
Film recorders   145
Filters
    defined   185
    in color scanner   29
    in early image-editing software   87
Flatbed scanners   33
    as competition for drum scanners   34
    defined   185
    resolution range   25

Forms
    software   120
Fractal Design   88
FrameMaker   114

G

Gamma curve   71
    applying   73
    defined   186
Gang scanning   31
Glass
    on flatbed scanner   40
Graphics accelerators   52
Gray scale
    bits of data in   10
    dithering   27
    trade off with resolution   128

H

Halftones   17
    color   133
    creating on output device   123
    defined   187
    line screens   19
    producing with output device   123
    traditional   133
Hand-held scanners   30
HiFi color   162
Highlights
    calibrating   70
Histogram
    function in image-editing software   101
HLS
    color model   14

I

IBM PC
    compatible computers   43
Illustration software   115
Image control
    function in PageMaker   109
Images
    categories of   8
    continuous tone   17
    importing   117
    types of   60
Imagesetters
    as output devices   129
    defined   187
    halftone dots   61
Imaging
    biological   7
Ink
    absorption of   18
Inkjet printers   123
Interfaces
    hardware   47
Internet
    as multimedia forum   119
Interpolation
    defined   188
    in scanners   26
IVUE
    format   90

J

JPEG
  compression   82
  defined   188

K

Kodak
  Photo CD   39

L

Large-format output   144–145
Laser Printers   126–129
Lasso
  tool in image-editing software   96
Legal issues
  in image reproduction   105
Letraset   87
Light
  frequencies of   12
Line art
  capturing   61
Line screen
  defined   188
  from output devices   123
  how derived   18
Lithography
  reproduction of continuous tone   18
Live Picture   90

M

Macintosh
  amount of RAM   51
  as scanning workstation   41
Magic wand
  tool in image-editing software   96
Magneto-optical
  drives   56
Masks
  selecting areas in image-editing
    software   95
MatchPrint   138
Memory
  addressing in 386 chip   44
  needed for image-editing software   104
  requirements of workstations   50
  virtual   195
Microsoft Windows. *See* Windows
Midtones
  identification of   69
Moire
  defined   189
  subject   135
Moire patterns
  cause of   62
Mouse
  use in GUI   42
Multimedia
  production firms   151
  use of scanned images   119

N

Negatives
  scanning with slide scanner   35

O

OCR
  accuracy   170
  applications of   166
  features of   168
  use of document feeder   34
Operating systems   45
OPI
  print server   108
Output
  categories of   122
  use of terminology   122

P

Page-description language
  defined   190
PageMaker   108
Paintbrush
  tool in image-editing software   93
Paper
  dot gain in   18
  resin coated   129
Pentium
  microprocessor   44
Photo CD
  as alternative to scanner   39
Photo Multiplier Tubes. *See* PMTs
Photoshop
  Limited Edition   89
PICT
  file format   77
Pixel
  defined   191
Plates
  printing   20
Platesetters   136
Plug-ins
  for Photoshop   88
PMTs
  as alternative to CCDs   25
Portable documents   176
PostScript. *See also* EPS
  description of   124
  interface to color copiers   123
  level 2   125
  original limitations of   125
PowerPC
  microprocessor   43
Prepress
  service bureaus   149
Price
  of digital cameras   39
  of drum scanners   37
Printers
  dye-sub   141
  inkjet   140
  laser   126
Printing
  terminology of   121
Processors
  Pentium   44
  PowerPC   43
  RISC   44
Proofs
  digital   156
  film-based   137

in traditional publishing   20
press   138

Q

QuarkXPress
    color management in   74
    use of images in   111

R

RAM
    requirements   51
Raster image processor
    defined   192
Rational tangent screening   134
Reflective color   12
Removable hard disks   55, 110
Resolution
    defined   193
    of CCD   25
    of drum scanners   36
    of imagesetters   134
    of laser printers   126
    of MacPaint images   86
    of slide scanners   35
    of video frame grabbers   38
    setting in scanner control software   65
    trade-off with gray scale   128
RGB
    color model   14
RISC
    technology   44
Rotate
    function in image-editing software   99

S

Saturation
    in HLS model   14
Scaling
    image   65
Screens
    color angles   133
    defined   193
    frequency   18, 123
    stochastic   133, 135
SCSI
    interface   48
Selection tools
    in image-editing softare   95
Separations. *See* Color separations
Service bureaus
    output of files   21
    selecting   157
    use of OPI   108
Shadows
    calibrating   70
Sharpen
    filter   97
Sharpness
    of interpolated images   26
Sheetfed scanners   32
Shuttles
    removable hard drives   57
Single-pass scanners   29
Skew
    scanning straight   15

Slide scanners   35
Software
    bundled with scanners   60
    forms   120
    illustration   115
    multimedia   119
    scanner control   62
Standards
    for calibration   70
    SWOP   75
Storage
    mass   53
SWOP
    standard   75
SyQuest
    removable hard disks   55

T

T-shirt transfers   143
Targets
    for calibration   70
TIFF
    file format   76
    support in OCR programs   169
    use in presentation programs   119
Toner
    in laser printer   126
Tools
    painting   92
Tracing
    scanned images   117
Transfer function   71
Transmissive color   12
Transparency
    option for flatbeds   34
Transparency scanners   36
TWAIN
    evolution of   60
Typography
    in traditional publishing   19

U

UCR
    defined   194
    description   103
Undercolor removal. *See* UCR
Unix   46

V

Video
    capture boards   38

W

Waterless printing   163
Windows
    image-editing software   90
    introduction of   45
Word processors
    graphics in   114